Grammar and Dictionary of the Yakama Language

From The
Library
of
Don B. Woodcock

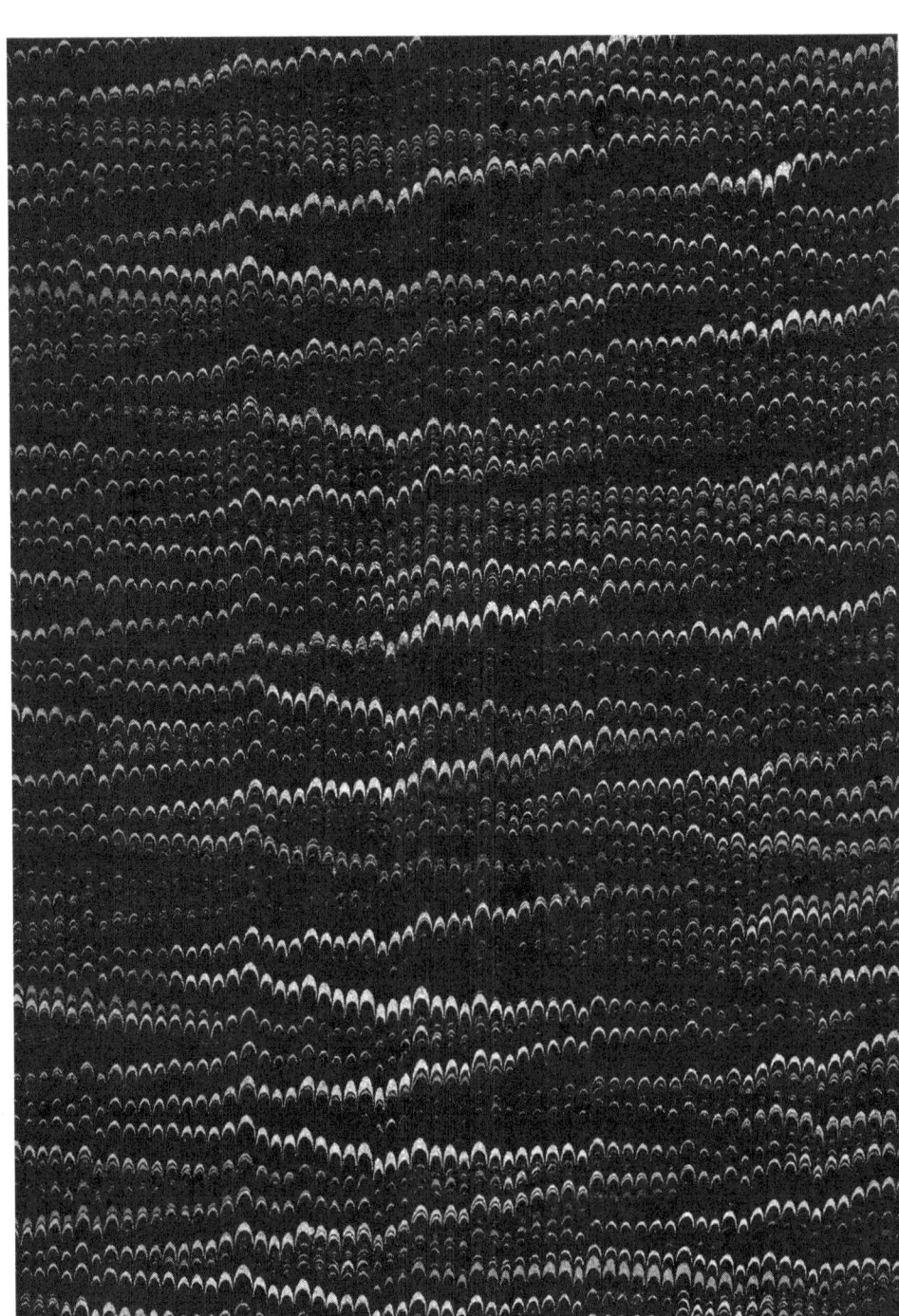

SHEA'S

LIBRARY OF AMERICAN LINGUISTICS.

VI.

GRAMMAR

AND

DICTIONARY

OF THE

YAKAMA LANGUAGE.

BY

REV M^{IE}. C^{LES}. PANDOSY,

OBLATE OF MARY IMMACULATE

TRANSLATED BY GEORGE GIBBS AND J G SHEA

NEW YORK
CRAMOISY PRESS
1862

Of 100 *copies printed*

No. 11 *[signature]*
Editor.

PREFACE.

The bands enumerated by Father Pandosy belong to the Sahaptin family of Mr Hale. This family he divides into two branches, the Sahaptin proper or Nez Percés, and the Walla-Walla, in which latter he includes all the others. The country occupied by them extends from the Dalles of the Columbia to the Bitter-Root mountains, lying on both sides of the Columbia and upon the Kooskooskie and Salmon Forks of Lewis' and Snake River, between that of the Selish family on the north, and of the Snakes on the south.

The Pshwanwappam bands usually called Yakamas, inhabit the Yakama river, a stream heading in the Cascade Range and emptying into the Columbia above the junction of the Snake. The word signifies "the Stony Ground," in allusion to the rocky character of their country. Roil-roil-pam is the Klikatat country, situated in the Cascade mountains north of the Columbia and west of the Yakamas. Its meaning is "the Mouse country," referring to a popular local legend. The name Walla-Walla is explained by Father Pandosy. The band so called occupy the country south of the Columbia and about the river of that name. The Tairtla, usually called Taigh, belong, as stated in the text, to the environs of the Des Chutes river which drains the eastern base of the Cascades, south of the Columbia, and the Palus, usually written Paloose, live between the Columbia and the Snake. All these bands are independent, and in fact, most of them are divided among several chiefs.

The author of this grammar, Father M. C. Pandosy, was for a number of years resident among the Yakamas, and became perfectly acquainted with their language. In the destruction of the mission by fire, during the Indian war in Oregon and Washington Territory, the original of the grammar was lost, and the following translation made some time previously alone remained. A revision of the dictionary, much more extensive than the accompanying, was destroyed at the same time. As the mission was then broken up and but little chance exists of any equally complete memorial of this language being prepared hereafter, these have been adopted as a most valuable contribution to our linguistics.

Grammatical notices of the Sahaptin or Nez Percé language, which differs from the Walla-Walla perhaps as the Portuguese from the Spanish were given by Mr Hale in his Ethnology of the U S Exploring Expedition, and reviewed by Mr Gallatin in the Transactions of the American Ethnological Society.

Father Pandosy explains the value of the letters which he employs, but it is necessary to observe that there is no true *r* in the language, and the letter when used represents the guttural sound of *ch* in the Scottish *loch* or German *ich*.

INDIAN GRAMMAR

OF THE

P'SHWAN-WA-PAM, WALA-WALA, TAIRTLA, ROIL-ROIL-PAM AND PALUS LANGUAGES

The grammar which I now present, and which I have written in the Pshwanwapam language, gives at the same time an account of the Walawala, Tairtla (Indians of the Des-Chutes river and its environs), Roilroilpam and Palus, for theirs is a single language divided into so many dialects, while fundamentally it is the same, and a great majority of the words do not allow of a separation. I have written it in the Pshwanwapam in preference to either of the other dialects, because it is more familiar to me, clearer and easier than the rest.

I take the liberty of making the remark, in passing, that many persons write the word Walla-Walla with four *l* s. I have even seen this orthography in books, but I find it entirely defective, because it alters the word in falsifying the pronunciation, and thus puts it out of the question to recognize the meaning. According to this orthography it should, it appears to me, be pronounced Wal-la-wal-la, and I have heard it thus pronounced, and so for a long time pronounced it myself, but when by a sufficiently long residence among the Indians, I was able to stammer their language well enough to make myself understood, I asked the meaning of this word, and they replied "*Atuanaki pa waniksha komanak tenmaman,*" "those Indians are called after the river." Thus the word *Atwan*, which among the Pshwanwapams signifies river, is rendered by the Wala-Walas and the Palus by *uana*. Further the Indians of all this neighborhood form the diminutive by repeating the substantive, changing *n* into *l*, giving the voice a different tone, putting the lips out in speaking and keeping them suspended around the jaw. In this way we have the word *Wana-uana*, which by the change of *n* into *l* gives *Wala-uala*, which should be pronounced very short, *Wălă-uălă* and not Walla-walla.

Of the Letters.

I have thought best before entering upon the subject to give a sketch of the letters which I have used in writing the Pshwanwapam language, that those who may chance to see this paper may, though distant enough from the Yakama country, in some sort hear the Indians themselves speak

The Yakama language contains but sixteen letters, *a, e, i, o, u, w, c, h, k, l, m, n, p, r, s, t*. These letters have the same sounds as in European languages. Thus *a, e, i, o, u* are pronounced absolutely as a Frenchman would pronounce them, and as with us these vowels are capable of receiving a certain modification of sound by means of accents. The vowel *u* is met with very rarely, and excepting two or three words in which alone it occurs, the Indians pronounce it with difficulty. The consonants have the same sound as in French, and to simplify the orthography are pronounced after the new mode of spelling introduced into France some years since, consequently instead of saying *ka, elle, éme*, we spell simply *ke, le, me*. The vowel *a* is always mute in these cases. The letter *h* is always strongly aspirated. The *r* is always pronounced strong and guttural, or as it is in the German language. (a).

Strictly, other consonants might be admitted into the Indian alphabet, but this does not appear necessary, and it would be contrary to the spirit of the age which seeks to reduce every thing to its most simple expression. It would even embarrass the orthography by uselessly overloading it. What necessity is there in fact for the letter *q* when we possess the *k*, for have not these two precisely the same sound [in French]. The same desire to simplify the spelling as much as possible has made me reject the *y* and the orthographic sign called *tréma* (dialysis). Their retention is in fact useless since it is admitted as a principle that the letter *i* preceded or followed by a vowel or between two vowels is always pronounced as if it was a *y* or an *ï*. I have also struck out the *x*, which with us has not always the same sound, since it is sometimes pronounced like *gs*, and sometimes like *ks*. As among the Indians of this neighborhood it would never represent the first sound, I prefer to use *ks* instead. It might be said indeed that by giving as a general rule in the Yakama language that *x* is always pronounced like *ks*, this letter might figure in their alphabet, but experience has convinced me that the establishment of a general rule is insufficient to overthrow a habit of pronunciation acquired in early education and strongly rooted. Suppose that some one wished to study the Pshwanwapam language—if he cast his eyes upon the word written *ik-siks*, would he not seize at first glance the true pronunciation, whereas, on the other hand if he found it written with an *x*, *ixsix*, would he not be naturally led to pronounce it *ig-sigs*, a pronunciation which would be altogether incorrect.

(a) The w is here used apparently as older French missionaries used the Greek character ȣ. As a consonant it answers to our w, as a vowel to oo.   J. G. S.

I employ *ch* in words which are pronounced like the Chinook *tchoko*, for I do not see how the *t* placed before *ch* can give to it the pronunciation which is attributed to it. Besides, why invent a novel mode of orthography? Is not the pronunciation to be represented by *tch* found elsewhere? The English language abounds with it and yet not a single word is written thus. Why then introduce characters which, without presenting anything new, have the defective advantage or rather the inconvenience of embarrassing the reader and writer by surplusage. It is much more simple to say that *ch* is pronounced always as in English words in which those letters are found. The same is the case with *sh*.

Of the Parts of Speech

Like the dead languages, that of the Pshwanwapam contains but [eight] parts of speech, viz. the substantive, adjective [pronoun], verb, adverb, preposition, conjunction and interjection. The article there is wanting, but the substantives, adjectives and pronouns have the precious advantage of being declinable. It must be remarked that the substantives as well as the adjectives and participles have no gender. They vary neither in the masculine nor feminine.

CHAPTER I

Of the Substantive.

Two numbers are found in the substantives, the singular and plural, or as there is no article in the Indian language there are terminations or cases which remove all difficulty as to the sense of the words which we hear, since this sense is fixed by a terminal sign. These terminations or cases are six in each number as in Latin. The dative, accusative and ablative have a double sign, one simple the other compound.

To decline a substantive, it is sufficient to add to the positive the termination *nem* to have the nominative. It is however necessary to remark that the positive is itself a nominative, and that the sign *nem* is employed only in certain cases. Custom alone can make its proper use understood. To form the genitive, the termination *nmi* is added to the positive. For the simple dative the termination *iow* must be added, but if the substantive concludes with the vowel *i* in the positive, one is retrenched for the sake of euphony. The compound dative is formed by adding *iou* to the genitive, preserving the rule of euphony and thus giving *nmiow*. The simple accusative is made by adding the termination *nan* to the positive, while for the compound it must be added to the genitive. The Palus and Wala-walas form their terminal sign in *na* instead of *nan* whether simple or compound. The vocative is nothing but the positive preceded by the exclamation *na*

YAKAMA GRAMMAR.

[*Nah!*] The ablative simple is formed by adding to the positive the termination *ei*, but for the compound it is necessary, as in the other cases, to add it to the genitive.

The general sign of the plural is *ma*, which is found in all the cases, so that to form the plural it is sufficient to add *ma* to the positive and we have the nominative. The genitive plural is formed by adding *mi* to the nominative of the same number, which gives *ma-mi*. The dative is formed by adding the sign *miow* to the nominative; the accusative by adding *man;* the vocative preserves the *na* of the singular taking the plural termination *ma*, and for the ablative the termination *miei* is added.

Note.—In the plural the accusative only takes the compound termination. This is formed by adding to the sign of the plural the termination of the compound accusative, which gives *ma-mi-nan*.

Examples.

1st *Simple termination,* taking for the positive *kussi,* horse.

SINGULAR.

nom.	kussi-nan	the horse.
gen.	kussi-nmi	of the horse.
dat.	kussi-ow	to the horse.
acc.	kussi-nan	the horse.
voc.	na kussi	oh horse!
abl.	kussi-ei	for the horse.

PLURAL.

nom.	kussi-ma	the horses.
gen.	kussi-ma-mi	of the horses.
dat.	kussi-ma-miow	to the horses.
acc.	kussi-ma-man	the horses.
voc.	na-kussi-ma	oh horses!
abl.	kussi-ma-miei	for the horses.

2d. *Compound termination,* taking for the positive miawar, *chief.*

SINGULAR.

nom.	miawar-nem	the chief.
gen.	miawar-nmi	of the chief.
dat.	miawar-nmi-iow	to the chief.
acc.	miawar-nmi-nan	the chief
voc.	na miawar	oh chief!
abl.	miawar-nmi-ei	for the chief.

PLURAL

nom	miawar-ma	the chiefs
gen	miawar-ma-mi	of the chiefs
dat	miawar-ma-miow	to the chiefs
acc	miawar-ma-man	the chiefs
voc	na miawar-ma	oh chiefs!
abl	miawar-ma-miei	for the chiefs

Sometimes for euphony a syncope is made in the plural, and this syncope affects all the cases except the nominative and the vocative

Example

nom	kussi-ma	the horses
gen	kussi-mi	of the horses
dat	kussi-miow	to the horses
acc	kussi-man	the horses
voc	na kussi-ma	oh horses!
abl	kussi-miei	for the horses

By the above example it will be seen that to form the syncope, it is sufficient in the genitive, dative, acusative and ablative, which are the only cases susceptible of being affected by it, it is sufficient, I say, to retrench the essentially plural termination ma. After this it is easy to conclude that the sign mi indicates always a genitive, that of iow a dative, that of an an accusative, and that of ei an ablative. These few directions suffice to decline all the substantives

Every substantive is capable of being changed into a verbal adjective *Exceptions*.—A large number of substantives. See hereafter

CHAPTER II

Of the Adjective.

Substantives having no gender, as we have said, it follows that the adjectives have none, but they are declinable and possess the same cases as substantives. Like the latter, adjectives take the signs of simple and of double agreement, or the compound termination

Every verbal adjective, whether present or past participle, is double, for it either affirms or denies. 1st, that the substantive is put in action, 2d, the presence or existence of the substantive

1st If we desire to affirm that the substantive is put in action, we adjectify it by adding to its positive the termination *tla*, for example *atawit*, love, adjective affirming action *atawit-la*, loving. If on the other hand we deny the action, we add to the positive the termination *al*, as *atawial*, unloving. When the positive is terminated by the letter *t*, *la* only is added instead of *tla*, as seen in the above example. This letter is also dropped to form the negative. Sometimes to obtain the negative *nal* instead of *al* is added, principally in those words which terminate in *m*, for example *tanamwtwm*, prayer, *tanamwtwmnal*, not praying. In words ending in *k* or *kt*, and in some Wala-wala words ending in *sha*, the negative verbal adjective is formed by adding *kal* to the termination of the positive.

2d If we wish to affirm that a thing is present or exists, we add to the positive the termination *ni* or *ié*. Example *timat*, [a] writing, *timani*, written, *twin*, tail, *twinié*, having a tail. If on the contrary we deny presence or existence, we add to the positive the sign *nal* or *nwt*. Example *timanal*, unwritten, *twinwt*, without a tail. But though this is the rule, it is necessary to remark that *twinwt* is not always used, but the *n* is replaced by *l*, as was mentioned in the beginning, making *twilwt*. For all other substantives *nwt* is used, unless we wish to cast ridicule upon the word, in which case we should make use of *lwt*.

Adjectives properly so called, as well as those derived from verbs (both affirmative and negative), and also participles are declined in the same manner as substantives.

Examples

1 *Simple*

SINGULAR

nom	shir-nem	*the good*
gen	shir-nmi	*of the good*
dat	shir-iow	*to the good*
acc	shir-nan	*the good*
voc	na-shir	*oh good!*
abl	shir-ei	*for the good*

PLURAL

nom	shir-ma	*the good, &c*
gen	shir-ma-mi	
dat	shir-ma-miow	
acc	shir-ma-man	
voc	na shir-ma	
abl	shir-ma-mei	

YAKAMA GRAMMAR.

2 Compound
SINGULAR

nom	chélwit	*the bad*
gen	chélwit-nmi	*of the bad, &c*
dat	chélwit nmiow	
acc	chelwit nminan	
voc	na chélwit	
abl	chélwit nmei	

PLURAL

nom	chelwit-ma
gen	chelwit-mami
dat	chelwit-mamiow
acc	chelwit-maminan
voc	na chelwit-ma
abl	chelwit-mamiei

Verbal Adjectives.

Simple
SINGULAR

nom	sh-nweitla-nem	*the compassionate.*
gen	sh-nweitla-nmi	*of the, &c*
dat	sh-nweitla-iow	
acc	sh-nweitla-nan	
voc	na sh-nweitla	
abl	sh-nweitla-iei	

PLURAL

nom	sh-nweitla-ma
gen	sh-nweitla-mami
dat	sh-nweitla-mamiow
acc	sh-nweitla-ma-man
voc	na-shnweitla-ma
abl	sh-nweitla-mamiei

Compound
SINGULAR

nom	sh-nweitla-nem
gen	sh-nweitla-nmi
dat	sh-nweitla-nmiow
acc	sh-nweitla-nminan
voc	na sh-nweitla
abl	sh-nweitla-nmiei

PLURAL.

nom.	sh-nweitla-ma
gen.	sh-nweitla-mami
dat.	sh-nweitla-mamiow
acc.	sh-nweitla-maminan
voc.	na sh-nweitla-ma
abl.	sh-nweitla-mamiei

The syncope which occurs sometimes in substantives is much more general with verbal adjectives. Thus, instead of saying in the acusative singular *sh-nweitla-nan, sh-nweitla-nminan,* we say *sh-nweitlan, sh-nweitla-minan.* In the plural by syncope we say in the genitive *sh-nweitla-mi;* in the dative *sh-nweitla-miow;* in the accusative *sh-nweitla-man;* in the ablative *sh-nweitla-miei.*

CHAPTER III.

Of the Pronoun.

The pronouns are very numerous and are declined, but their mode of declension is peculiar to them.

§ 1. OF THE PERSONAL PRONOUN.

1st. *Personal pronoun 1st person*, or the one who performs the action expressed by the verb.

SINGULAR.

nom.	ink, nes or nesh, sh	*I.*
gen.	enmi	*of me.*
dat.	enmiow	*to me.*
acc.	inak	*me*
voc.	(wanting)	
abl.	enmiei	*for me.*

PLURAL.

nom.	namak, natés, nanam, aatés, namtk,	*we.*
gen.	néémi	*of us.*
dat.	néémiow	*to us.*
acc.	némanak	*us.*
abl.	néémiei	*for us.*

2d person, that is to say the one spoken to.

SINGULAR

nom	ımk, nam	thou
gen	émink, més or mésh	of thee
dat	émıwk	to thee
acc	ımanak	thee
abl	émıeı or émıkaıéı	for thee

PLURAL

nom	ımak, pam, matés	you
gen	(wantıng)	of you
dat	émamıwk	to you
acc	ımmanak	you
abl	émmıeı	for you

In all cases where the personal pronouns termınate ın *ak* among the Pshwan-wapams, the Wala-walas and Palus drop the *k*, thus they say ın the accusatıve sıngular of the first persou *ına*, ın the nomınatıve plural *nama*, ın the accusatıve of the same number *namana*. It ıs the same ın the other persons, but ıt must be notıced that ın the accusatıve plural of the second person, ınstead of sayıng *ımanak*, they express themselves thus *émımanak*

3d person or the one spoken of

SINGULAR

	Pshwanwapam		Wala-Wala and Palus
nom	Penk	he	Penk (*some do not pronounce the k*)
gen	pın-mınk	of hım	pınmın
dat	pın-mıwk	to hım	pınmıow
acc	pın-mın	hım	pınmınnan
abl	pın-mıkaıéı	for hım	pınmıeı

PLURAL

nom	pmak	they	pma
gen	pé-mınk	of them	pamın
dat	pé-mıwk	to them	pamıwk
acc	pé-mınak	them	pamanak
abl	pé-mıkaıeı	for them	pamıkaıeı

The Indıans of the Falls (Taır) ınstead of the termınatıon *ak*, have ın their pronouns, and even ın their adverbs, that of *eı*. Thus they say, personal pronoun, 1st person, accusatıve sıngular, *ıneı*, nomınatıve plural *nameı*, accusatıve *némaneı*, pronoun of the 2d person, acc sıng *ımaneı*, nom plur *ımeı*, acc *ımaneı* or *emımaneı*, pronoun of 3d person, nom plur *p-meı*, acc *pamaneı*

It wıll be seen by the above declensıons that the personal pronouns are very numerous among the Indıans, partıcularly ın certaın cases, as the nominatives, but they cannot be employed indifferently, and the knowledge of their proper use is difficult to acquire. To aid in arriving the more easily at this knowledge, I have thought best to give the following table.

1st. Pronoun personal in the nominative case.

SINGULAR

1st person	ink, nes, sh,	*I*
2d person	imk, nam,	*thou*
3d person	penk, i,	*he*

PLURAL

1st person	namak, natés, nanam, namtk, tésh,	*we*
2d person	pam, imak, matés, amatés,	*you*
2d person	p-mak, pa, pat,	*they*

When the personal pronoun serves to designate the person who speaks, the pronoun in the nominative case is used, and is always placed before the verb if expressed by *ink*, *nés*. Example: I sing, *ink nés wempsha*, I speak, *ink nes nattwnsha*. The personal pronoun can be rendered by *ink* only, but *ink*, *nés* is more elegant and more in the Indian spirit, though it is a pleonasm banished from our European languages. The same pleonasm is found again in the other persons, as well singular as plural. If instead of *ink nes* we use *sh* only it is put at the end of the word, as *nattwnshesh* I speak, *wempshesh* I sing. Some bands do not aspirate the *h* in this last case and say simply *nattwnshes*, *wempshés*. In negative phrases *nes* is commonly used alone and placed immediately after the negative. Ex. I know nothing about it *chaw nés ashwkwasha*, I will not sing *chaw nés wempta*. In some cases, however, when it is wished to give more force to the reply, *ink* is used, but preceded by *nés* as *chaw nes ink*, it is not I.

In phrases conveying interrogation or doubt *nés* alone is used, as *mish nés winata*, shall I go, *kwak nés mish*, perhaps I will go, perhaps not. In ironical expressions both are used, the verb of the action being placed between the two. Ex. *wish nes winatarnei ink*, shall I go? a phrase corresponding to the French, "as tu le courage de penser que j'irai (pour toi)?"

When we wish to give force to an idea *ink nés* is used and expressed together, succeeded by the verb, which again is followed by the pronoun *ink*. *Ink nes nattwnsha-ink*, I myself speak.

In the first person plural *namak* is employed, either alone or accompanied by *natés* or *natesh*, placed together or with several words between the two at will. Examples, *namak nates ania nit*, we made the house, *namak natés wempta*, we will sing. In negative phrases *tés* and *natés* are used indifferently, which are joined to the negative. Example we do not laugh, *chaw tés tiasha* or *chaw nates tiasha*. If it is wished to give more force *namak* is added. *Nanam* is employed only when two persons are spoken of, whilst *namtk* expresses always a great number. Example *napınık nanam wınata*, we two will go, *aw namtk atsha*, let us go.

2d. Pronoun personal in the accusative case.

SINGULAR

1st person	ınak nés, ınak nam,	me
2d person	ımanak més, ımanak nam,	thee
3d person	pénık ı, kônak ı,	him

PLURAL

1st person	némanak,	us
2d perssn	ımmanak,	you
3d person	pémanak kômanak.	them

When the personal pronoun is in the accusative case *ınak* can be used alone in the first person or *nés* added at will. Ex. *ınak ınatonosha* or *ınak nes ınatonosha*, he chides me.

§ 2. THE POSSESSIVE PRONOUN

First Person

SINGULAR

nom	enmı	my, mine
gen	enmı,	of my
dat	enmıow,	to my.
acc	enmın,	my (in Wala-wala and Palus *enmına*.)
voc	na enmı,	oh my
abl	enmıeı, enmı kaıeı,	by my

PLURAL

nom	enmıma,	my, mine

There is no other plural case, for as it is evident that the possessive is nothing but the personal pronoun, the accusative only changes.

2d person, nom *emınk*, thy, thine, acc *emın* or *emıan*. There is no plural.
3d person, is absolutely like the third person of the personal pronoun.

Singular of the First Person Plural

			Wala Wala and Palus
nom	nèémı,	our,	naamı
gen	nèémı,	of our,	naamı
dat	neémıow,	to our,	naamıow
acc	nèémın,	our,	naamına
voc	na nèémı,	oh our,	na naamı
abl	nèémıeı,	by our,	naamıeı

There is no plural.

Singular of 2d Person Plural

nom	mamınk,	your,	mamın
gen	"	of your,	"
dat	mamıwk,	to your,	mamıow
acc	mamın,	your,	mamına
voc	na mamınk,	oh your,	na mamın
abl	mamı-kaıéı,	by your,	mamıeı

There is no plural

Singular of 3d Person Plural

nom	pénınk,	their,	pamın
gen	"	of their,	"
dat	pémıwk,	to their,	pamıow
acc	pémın,	their,	pamınaı
voc	na pémınk,	oh their	na pamın,
abl	pémıkaıeı,	by their	pamıeı

Sometimes the possessive pronouns, my, thy, are rendered by their corresponding personals, me, thee, when friendship or relationship is expressed Thus, instead of saying *enmı, réı, emınk réı*, my friend, thy friend, we say *ınk reı, ım reı*, me friend, thee friend, *ınkoten, ın pıtz*, me son, me nephew, instead of *enmı koten, enmı pıtz*

§ 3 INTERROGATIVE PRONOUN

SINGULAR.

nom	shın, (*some tribes say*) shın,			who, what which
gen	shımın,	"	shınnmı,	of whom
dat	shımıow,	"	shınnmıow,	to whom
acc	shımıan (*comp* shımınan) shımınan,			whom
voc				
abl	shımıeı,		shınmıeı,	by whom

PLURAL

nom	shımen The other cases are not used

CHAPTER IV

Of the Verb.

The verbs have only certain tenses, viz indicative imperfect or past pluperfect, future, conditional, imperative, infinitive, present and past participles, gerund

YAKAMA GRAMMAR.

CONJUGATION OF THE VERBS TO HAVE AND TO BE

1st TO HAVE (avoir)

Indicative Present

nesh wa *or* wash nesh,	*I have*
mesh wa *or* wash mesh,	*thou hast*
penk awa *or* pinmink awa,	*he has*
natésh wa *or* wash natésh,	*we have*
matesh wa *or* wash matésh,	*you have*
pa wa *or* pemink awa,	*they have*

In these verbs there is but one mode of expressing the past and the pluperfect

Past and Pluperfect

nesh wacha,	*I had or have had*
mesh wacha,	*thou hadst, &c*
awacha,	*he had*
natésh wacha,	*we had*
matésh wacha,	*ye had*
awacha,	*they had*

Future

nesh } wata mesh }	*I shall* } *have* *thou shalt* }
awata,	*he shall have*
natesh } wata, matesh }	*we shall* } *have* *ye shall* }
p' awata,	*they shall have*

The verb to have has no imperative

Conditional

nesh } watarnei, mesh }	*I should* } *have* *thou shouldst* }
awatarnei,	*he should have*
natésh } watarnei, matésh }	*we should* } *ye should* } *have*
watarnei,	*they should* }

2d TO BE (Etre)

Indicative Present

ink nésh wa,	*I am*
imk nam wa,	*thou art*
penk iwa,	*he is*
namak natésh, nanam, namtk wa,	*we are*
imak pam wa,	*you are*
pmak pa wa,	*they are*

Past and Pluperfect

ınk nesh wacha,	*I was, have or had been*
ımk nam wacha,	*thou wast, &c*
penk ıwacha,	*he was*
natesh wacha, nanam, namtk, namak,	*we were*
matésh wacha,	*you were*
p-mak pawacha,	*they were*

Future

ınk nesh wata,	*I will be*
ımk nam wata,	*thou wilt be*
penk ıwata,	*he will be*
namak natesh, nanam, namtk, wata,	*we will be*
ımak pam wato,	*you will be*
pa wata,	*they will be*

Imperative

awak,	*be thou*
awatk,	*be ye, let them be*

Conditional

ınk nésh ⎫	
ımk nam ⎬ waternei,	*I should be, &c*
penk ı ⎭	
namak natesh, nanam namtk ⎫	
pmak pa ⎬ watarnei,	

§ 2. Of the Active Verb.

All the tenses of the active verb are formed from the infinitive, which always terminates in *sha* or in *ra*

The indicative present preserves the infinitive termination *sha* or *ra*, but the first two persons of the singular and plural nevertheless may take a particular termination These are even employed by preference when the phrase is affirmative or interrogative In these cases the personal pronouns which precede the verbs are dropped, or rather are added to the termination These pronouns are *és* or *ésh* for the first, *am* for the second person singular, *tesh* for the first, and *pam* for the second person plural When the pronouns are placed after the verb, in order to avoid the hiatus which would occur by approximating the final *a* and the initial *é*, *a* an elision is made by dropping the final vowel of the infinitive There are a great number of other finals, but as these are not common to all the words, I omit them here, as, in order to indicate them, it would be necessary to make a particular nomenclature of all these terminations and of the verbs to which they are adapted

The past is formed by changing the termination of the infinitive *sha*, *ra* into *na*

The pluperfect is formed by adding the monosyllable *na* to the infinitive termination *sha*

The future is formed by changing the termination of the infinitive into *ta*

The conditional is made by substituting for the infinitive termination that of *arna* or *tarnei*. The Walla-wallas, Roilroilpaius and Palus instead of *tarnei* use *tarna*

The present participle is formed by changing the infinitive termination *sha* into *tla* for the affirmative, and *nal* for the negative; the past participle by changing it to *ie*, *nié*, *ni* for the affirmative, and into *nwt*, *nal* for the negative

The gerund is obtained by changing *sha* into *tésh* or *tés*, or into *nat*, or still again *anat* if the last letter of the root is an *i*

The imperfect is only the past preceded by the preposition *irwé* later, scarcely (Walla-walla *arwé*)

The pluperfect is sometimes rendered by the past, but the verb must then be preceded by the adverb *miwi* (Walla-walla *mimi*) a long time

The imperative is formed by changing the *sha* of the infinitive into the letter *k* for the singular and *tk* for the plural

CONJUGATION OF THE ACTIVE VERB

Infinitive,	timasha,	to write
Participles present,	timatla,	writing, fond of writing
	timanal,	not writing.
Participles past,	timani,	written
	timanal,	unwritten
Gerund,	timatés / timanat	for writing

Indicative Present

ink nés timasha,	I write
imk nam timasha,	thou writest
penk i timasha,	he writes
namak natés, / nanam, namtk, } timasha,	we write
imak pam timasha,	you write
pa timasha,	they write

Second form

timashés,	I write or do I write
timashain,	thou writest or dost thou write
i timasha,	he writes or does he write
timashatés,	we write or do we write
timashapan,	you write or do you write
pa timasha,	they write or do they write

Past

Ink nes timana,	*I have written*
imk nam timana,	*thou hast written*
penk i timana,	*he has written*
namak natés timana,	*we have written*
imak pam timana,	*ye have written*
pa timana,	*they have written*

Second form

timanés,	*I have written or have I written*
timanam,	*thou hast written or hast thou written*
i timana,	*he has written or has he written*
timanatés,	*we have written or have we written*
timanapam,	*ye have written or have ye written*
pa timana,	*they have written or have they written*

Pluperfect.

ink nes timashana,	*I had written*
imk nam timashana,	*thou hadst written*
penk i timashana,	*he had written*
namak nates, &c , timashana,	*we had written*
imak pam timashana,	*ye had written*
pa timashana,	*they had written*

Second form

timashanés,	*had I written*
timashanam,	*hadst thou written*
i timashana,	*had he written*
timashana tés,	*had we written*
timashana pam,	*had ye written*
pa timashana,	*had they written*

Future.

ink nés timata,	*I shall or will write*
imk nam timata,	*thou shalt or wilt write.*
penk i timata,	*he shall or will write*
namak nates, &c , timata,	*we shall or will write.*
imak pam timata,	*ye shall or will write*
pa timata,	*they shall or will write*

Second form

timatés,	*shall I write?*
timatam,	*wilt thou write?*
itimata,	*will he write?*
timatatés,	*shall we write?*

tımatapam,	*will ye write?*
pa tımata,	*will they write?*

Conditional

ınk nes tımatarneı,	*I should or would write*
ımk nam tımatarneı,	*thou shouldst or wouldst write*
penk ı tımatarneı,	*he should or would write*
namak natés, &c , tımatarneı,	*we should or would write*
ımak pam tımatarneı,	*ye should or would write*
pa tımatarneı,	*they should or would write*

Second form

In this there is an irregularity which runs through all the verbs

tımatarneınes,	*should I write*
tımatarneınam,	*shouldst thou write*
ı tımaturneı,	*should he write,*
tımatarneınatés,	*should we write*

Imperative

sing	tımak or amash tımak,	*write*
plur	tımatk or amatésh tımatk,	*write ye*

§ 3. The Passive Verb.

The passive verb is only the present or past participle or the gerund, conjugated with the auxiliaries to have or to be according to the necessity of the case

Example

Indicative present

Tımatla	nesh wa,	*I am writing*
"	mesh wa,	*thou art writing*
"	awa,	*he is writing.*
"	natesh, nanam, namtk wa,	*we are writing*
"	matesh wa,	*ye are writing*
"	pa wa,	*they are writing,*
Tımanı	nesh wa,	*I am written*
"	nam wa,	*thou art written*
"	ıwa,	*he is written.*
"	natesh, nanam, namtk wa,	*we are written*
"	pam wa,	*ye are written*
"	pa wa,	*they are written*

It is the same with all the tenses, but it must be remarked that in the passive there is no infinitive

§ IV. Of the Personal Verb.

The personal verb is formed by putting before the active verb expressing the mode of being which it is intended to express, the disyllable *pina* for the persons of the singular, and *pima* for those of the plural. Sometimes *piné, pime* are employed instead, when the verb to which the disyllable is joined, commences with a vowel, but *pina, pima* may be used.

Example

Infinitive

pina tkrersha,	*to love oneself*

Participle present

pina tkrertla,	*loving oneself*
pina tkrernal,	*not loving oneself*

Participle past

pina tkrerni,	*to have loved oneself*

Gerund.

pina tkrertésh } pina tkreranat }	*of loving oneself*

Indicative Present

ink nesh ⎫		*I love myself*
imk nam ⎬	pima tkrersha,	*thou lovest thyself*
penk i ⎭		*he loves himself*
namak-natesh, &c, ⎫		*we love ourselves*
imak pam ⎬	pima tkrersha.	*ye love yourselves*
p-mak-pa ⎭		*they love themselves*

Second form

pina tkrershés,	*I love myself, &c.*
pina tkrersham,	
i pina tkrersha,	
pima tkrershatés,	
pima tkrershapam,	
pima tkrershapat,	

Past

ink nesh ⎫ imk nam ⎬ pina tkrerna, penk i ⎭	
namak-natesh ⎫ imak pam ⎬ pima tkrerna. p-mak pa ⎭	

Second form.

pına tkernés,
pına tkrernam,
ı pına tkrerna,
pıma tkrernatés,
pıma tkernapam,
pıma tkrernapat,

It is the same in all the other tenses

§ V. Of the Reciprocal Verb.

The active verb is also used to form the reciprocal verb, being preceded by the dissyllable *papa* In the third person plural, however, where *pa* is found it is dropped, doubtless, for euphony These verbs have no singular

Example

Indicative present

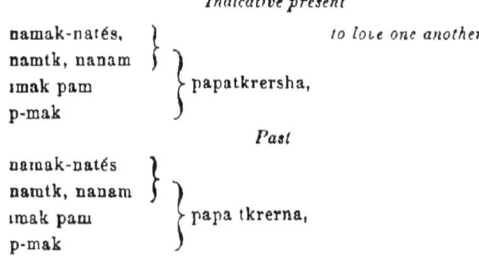

namak-natés, }
namtk, nanam } }
ımak pam   } } papatkrersha,
p-mak   }

Past

namak-natés }
namtk, nanam } }
ımak pam   } } papa tkrerna,
p-mak   }

These two tenses will suffice to aid in conjugating the others, since, as will be seen, it is enough to place *papa* between the pronouns and the verb and to conjugate the latter in the active voice

§ VI. Of Compound Verbs.

The compound verbs are very numerous, but the following are the cases of composition

1 If it is desired to express an action done or said far from the place where we are, and which in the idea implies motion, the compound is formed by adding *msh* to the ordinary terminations of the indicative For the past the radical *na* is changed into *ma* Ex *tımasha, tımashamsh , tımana, tıma-ma* For the pluperfect *shana* is changed into *shama* , for the future *m* is placed before the termination *ta* , *tımata, tımamta* , for the conditional *m* is placed before the sign *tarnet* , *tımatarnet, tımamtarnet* , for the imperative *m* is substituted for or placed before *k*, as *tımak, tımam , tımatk tımamtk* In this case the verb expresses motion from a distance towards the speaker, whether the person spoken of has himself moved or has caused the move-

ment directly or indirectly   Ex he has written to me, *itimana*, he has come to write *itimama*

2 If an action is to be expressed which require motion from the place where one is towards a distant one, the syllable *ta* is used between the root and the terminal sign, and the verb is conjugated according to the examples above given   Ex he has gone to write, *itimatana*, he will go to write, *itimatata*, go write *timatak*

3 If the compound verb is preceded in French by the verb "finir," the verb which expresses the action is rendered by its substantive, which is followed by the Indian verb to finish, *nakrisha*   Example, I cease to write, *timat nakriska*, and the verb *nakrisha* alone is conjugated, as I will stop writing *timat nakrites*

4 If the compound verb is preceded in French by the verb "faire," this last is expressed by *shapa* or by *téi*, which is placed before the root, and the verb is conjugated in the usual manner as, I will set you to writing (Je te ferai écrire) in a moment, *kliks mesh shapa-timata*

5 If we wish to express disdain, irony, &c , the syllable *tra* or *kra* is placed before the verb which indicates the idea to be conveyed   Example, he has written badly *itratimana*, he has written against his will &c

6 To mark the frequent repetition of an act by the same person, a continuity which excludes all other occupation, the termination *simisa* is added to the substantive which conveys the idea to be expressed, and *simisa* is conjugated as an active verb   Ex he does nothing but write, he writes all the time, *itimatat simisa*, he will do nothing but write, *itimatat simita*

7 If we desire to express an action, fugitive, momentary, or of short duration, the monosyllable *we* is used before the verb, and the latter is conjugated according to the usual rule, as I will write for a moment, *as we timata*, he has written a few words *awtika iwetimana*

8 To convey a longer duration, a long space of time, *tama* is placed before the verb   Ex I have waited long for you, *lekwi mésh tamawaria*, I will wait a long time for you, *lekwi més tamawcarita*   *Lekwi* and *tama* are in fact a pleonasm, for *lekui* itself signifies a long time   It can at pleasure be used or dropped

9 If an action is to be expressed which is done during the night, *taw* is made use of before the verb   *tawtimashés* I write in the night time, *itaw timana*, he wrote at night

Examples

I pina - shapa - taw - tra - hlik - tama warsha
He himself makes night disagreeably tiresome long wait, he keeps one long waiting for him at night   Pina, personal, shapa, *make one do*, taw, *something happening at night*, tama, *a thing indicating a length of time*, tra, *something disagreeable*, hlik, *something tiresome*, wet, *a thing of short duration*

I pina pitlasha, *he washes himself*

I shapa winasha, *he makes one go*
I taw wempsha, *he sings at night*
I tra washasha, *he goes disagreeably on horseback (cannot ride)*
I we wempta, *he will sing little (he will sing only a moment);* hlik nam nattwanha, *you speak tediously, (you are a tiresome talker)*, am, *to do a thing for some one*, klakem am auim, *make me a saddle*

Syntax.

The syntax in the Indian language is very simple.

1st The Government of the Substantive

The government of the substantive is indicated by the genitive, that is to say, every substantive governs the genitive. Ex Peter's book (the book of Peter) *Pierre-mni timas* The wooden house (the house of wood) *elwkasnmi nit* As will be observed the governed is always placed before the substantive which governs it

If the governing substantive is itself governed by a verb, the substantive which it governs takes the compound termination, and is put in the same case as that which governs it The compound terminal sign is only the union of the dative or accusative with the genitive Example, I am going to the chief's house, *miawarnmiow nitiow nes uinasha*, I am going to the governor's house, *tamanwitlanmiou nitiow winashes*, I execute my father's orders, *na totasanminun tamanwitnan nes twanasha*

2d. Agreement of Verbs.

Verbs agree with each other, that is to say, if the principal verb or the one which expresses the first idea is in the present, all the others will also be in the present, if in the future, they all take the future sign, if in the conditional, they will all be in the conditional tense This is always to be understood of the verbs which relate to the principal verb Ex If I had gone there and had seen you, I would have engaged you to have accompanied me (si j'y etais allé et que je te visse je t'aurai engagé a m accompagner) *paish nes winatarnei ko mes kreinu tarnei, narawtarnei mes tuanatiowi-
si je irai et je verrai engagerai te accompagne-
nak
ment-moi* A literal translation

3d. Agreement of Prepositions.

When a word is governed by a preposition or joined to one, all the substantives which refer to it take the preposition in like manner Ex He is in my house, *enmipa nitpa iwa* (my in house, in he is) He was hurt in mounting a skittish horse, *wieichutlaki kussiki isapneika* (ombrageux par cheval, par il s'est blessé)

Remark.

In elevated style (for the Indians also have the common style and the elevated in their oratory), they keep the noun governed by the verb in the positive, as if indeclinable, and yet put in the accusative the adjectives and pronouns depending on the substantive governed by the verb. It is by virtue of this rule that they say imanak patmaknanitarnei wanicht instead of patmaknanitarnei eminan wanichtan. In these cases, as will be observed in the Lord's Prayer, the possessive pronoun is replaced by the personal Ex. nemanak nim tkwatat instead of nim neeminan tkwatatnan, &c.

SPECIMENS OF THE YAKAMA LANGUAGE

Nĕĕmı Psht, ımk năm w̌ămsh Roĭemĭch-nik, shir
Our Father thou thou art high on the side (heaven), well

(năm 'mănăk*) p'a ť-măknăuı tărnēı wănĭcht́, shir ĕw̄ĭănă-
thou they (indef) should respect the name well should

witărneī ĕw̄ĭnk mıawarwıt, shir nammanak pa tw̌ănĕnıtărnĕı,
arrıve thy chieftaınshıp, well thee they (ınd) should follow

ichīnăk tēchămpă, tēumă, prwī. (ămăkwsrĭmmănăk*) pă
here earth (on), inhabıtants (the), will, thou as thyself they

tw̌ănenĭshămsh roĭemipămă tenmă Nēmănăk nĭm
follow, high of the (heaven) inhabıtants (the) Our (us) give us

ť-kw̌atăk kw̌alĭssĭm maısı maısı Nēmănăk laknănĭm chĕlwitĭt:
food always to-morrow to-morrow Our (us) forget sıns

ăătēskw̄sri nămăk ť-nōrmămăn laknăuĭshă chĕlwitĭt anakwnkink
us as we others forget sing have by whıch

nĕĕmĭow̄ pă chĕlwitĭă R-ť-to ănıănim nēmănăk tĕmnă,
us have offended Strong make our (us) heart,

ť-krăw̄ krĭal Nēmănăk eĭkrēnkĕm chĕlwit-ǩnik
(that ıt fall not) Us snatch bad from the sıde (from evıl)

Ekw̄s īwă nĕĕmī tĕmnă
So ıt is our heart

---

* Năm manak This is produced by the elision of na ımanak! O thou' The employment of the exclamation na is an elegance, and at the same time shows both greater respect and stronger desire

† Amakwsrımmanak, elision between amakwsrı and ımmanak It is to be noted that kwsrı, as, in the same manner, just as, requires to be preceded by a sign indicating the person who acts or, at least, is the soul of the action Ex Es kwsrı ınk, (I) as I, amukwsrı ımk, (thou) as thou, amakwsrı penk, (he) as he, ăstĕskwsrı namak, (we) as we, apam kwsrı ımak, (you) as you, anakwsrı pa, (they) as they

PEACE SONG COMPOSED BY FATHER PANDOSY

Air Marseillaise

I

Amatesh ımak klarma tenma	Allez vous tous (les) Sauvages (les)
Amatesh néman wınanôm	Allez, nous, venez, rejoindre
Klap-ré paleı pam tranana	Quoıque ınsensés vous soyez devenus
Apamko némanak nattwn	Lorsque vous nous parole
Wrınanıa kreshem-wıtkı	Avez rejeté entètement par
Kopam ıchı ıkwak paınta	Eh bıen ! vous maıntenant deviendrez docıles
Aow kwelh aow suıapônan	C'est assez l'Amérıcaın
Chélwıtpam alıônemta temna	Mauvaıs vous gager le cœur
Larstweı natesh wa Ténın Swıapoın	Un seul nous sommes Sauvages, Amérıcaıns
Epapnatesh papanısha Ténın Swıapoın	La maın nous nous donnons Sauvages, Amérıcaıns

II.

Aowpam ımmanak panıroıeıtkı	Eh bıen, vous, vous paıx par
Inarawshamsh kwır klamıtornı	Engage blanche tête
Amatesh aweıertıônem	Allez donc courez vers luı
Temna kto ananénım	Cœur vıte allez luı porter
Iaıama, Pıtrma, l'ımrma	Aınés (les), oncles (les), paternels, oncles (maternels)
Tılama, Pwshama, nekama	Grand pere, paternels, maternels, nos cadets
Aow klarma paanırweıtamta	Allons tous, venez, faıre la paıx
Shır pam alıônemta tenına	Bon vous engagerez cœur
Lars tweı tésh wata Ténın Swıapoın	Un seul nous serons Sauvages, Amécans
Epap, épap papaınta Ténın Swıapoın	La maın nous donnerons, Sauvages, Amérıcaıns

III

E, aow nam Colonel Wrıght, ımksa,	Ouı, eh ! bıen toı, Colonel Wrıght, toı seul,
Temnan nam pa ıshnanıa	Cœur le toı a gagné
Amako shırkı nattwnkí	Lorsque toı bonne par parole par

PEACE SONG.

Paanırweit nam pa swswnma	La paix tu nous a fait entendre à nos oreilles
Aow ko natesh nwitkaki éki	Eh! bien et nous, vrai par oui par (par un oui véritable)
Twimpesnan a-tkwei-ika	Le fusil avons posé à terre,
Kotesh émik-nink simka	Et nous de ton coté seulement
Ko imtwalrarmiow krepta	Et à ton ennemi tirerons
Lars twei natesh wa Ténin Swiapoin	Un seul nous sommes Sauvages et Américains
Epap natesh papanisha Swiapoin	La main nous nous donnons Sauvages, Américains

IV.

Anakopenk nam n'eémiow	Celui qui toi à nous
Imanak inichatama	Toi est venu amener
N'eémipa kopenk rairwit	Dans nous ce jour
Wakrish kwalisim iwata,	Vivant toujours sera
Woptashié tranak nattwn	Ailée devions parole
Aowlak aowlakpeink k-tôki	Dans le vide vite par
Klarmamiow nam weinatki	A tous les toi vol par
Paishtam Swiapomamiow	l'araitras aux Américains
Lars twei natesh wa Ténin Swiapoin	Un seul nous sommes, &c
Epap natesh papanisha Ténin Swiapoin	

V

Na reli rasloié chawalôks!	O colorié, étoilé drapeau!
Emipenk tesh lesetasa,	Dans toi nous nous plaçons (nous nous mettons sur les rangs)
Nééenuci ka nam wata.	
Papaiwm-mitpama timash	Pour nous aussi tu seras
Shirnam némanak naknwimta	Ralliement (de) signe
Amakwsri nam naknwitha.	Bien, toi, nous viendras garder
Klarmaman swiapómaman	De la meme manière que tu gardes tous les Américains
Emik nink tesh kliawita	
Lars twei natesh wa Ténin Swiapoin	De ton coté nous serons tués
Epap natesh papanisha Ténin Swiapoin	Un seul nous sommes, &c

I

Allons donc vous tous Sauvages, venez vous joindre à nous, quoique par votre entêtement à rejeter nos paroles, vous ayez fait une faute, du moins en ce moment soyez dociles à notre invitation C'est assez avoir un mauvais cœur contre les Américains Maintenant Sauvages et Américains nous ne sommes plus qu'un seul, Sauvages et Américains nous nous donnons la main

PEACE SONG.

II

Allons donc vous tous que la Tête Blanche engage, allons donc, courez vers lui, allez vite lui porter votre cœur, vous tous nos frères ainés, nos oncles (paternels, maternels) nos grands pères (paternels, maternels) et vous nos frères cadets, venez tous faire la paix, venez donner votre cœur Sauvages et Américans nous ne serons plus qu'un seul cœur, nous nous donnerons la main.

III

Oui, c'est toi et toi seul, Colonel Wright, qui as gagné nos cœurs lorsque par ta douce parole, que tu as fait entendre à nos oreilles, tu nous a engagé a la paix, c'est en toute verité que disant oui à ta proposition, nous avons déposé nos armes à terre pour ne les reprendre et n'en faire usage que sous tes ordres et contre tes ennemis Maintenant Sauvages et Américains, nous ne sommes plus qu'un seul cœur, Sauvages et Américains nous nous donnons la main

IV

Le jour qui ta conduit au milieu de nous vivra toujours dans notre cœur, ô ma parole prends tes ailes et d'un vol rapide va raisonner aux oreilles de tous les Américains maintenant Sauvages et Americains, nous ne sommes plus qu'un seul cœur, &c

V

O drapeau coloré et étoilé (drapeau Américain) nous nous plaçons sous ta protection, pour nous aussi tu seras un signe de ralliement, tu étendras sur nous aussi tes soins bienveillans comme tu les étends sur tous les Américains, et comme eux nous mourons pour ta défense Maintenant Sauvages et Américains nous ne sommes plus qu'un seul cœur, &c

DICTIONARY.

DICTIONARY.

Abandon, w-ré-sha, *p* wre-na, *f* w-ré-ta, *imp* a-w-renk *c* w-re-tar-nei

Abdomen, na-w-at

Abhor, *to,* shi-wa-sha, shana, shata, shak, tarnei, shiwet-no-sha, shana, ta, nak, tarnei

Able, wap-sor

Abominable, che-lw-it-nenk, mel-la-nenk

Abortion, n-mw-it, *to have an abortion,* n-mw-i-sha, na, ta, k, tar-nei

Above, rœmi *Gen* ché-nik, *acc and dat* chén, *from above,* rœmi-pama

Abstain, *to,* chaw-a-kw-sha, shana, akwta, akwk, akwtarnei

Abundance, lar-wit, *in abundance,* ma-aw

Abundant, lar, pa-la-lei

Abyss, krar

Accept, *to,* w-nep-sha, w-né-pa, w-nép-ta, w-nepk, tarnei

Accompany, *to,* twa-na-sha, nana, nata, nak, tarnei

Accustom, *to, one's self,* shir-tra-na-sha, na, ta, k, tarnei, shir-w-sha-ik-sha, a, ta, om, tarnei

Acorn, wo-wa-chi

Act, *an,* kwt-kwt

Act, *to,* a-kw-sha

Actually, ma-ké

Add, *to, (give over and above,)* shar-sha, na, ta, kuk, tarnei

Adder, pi-w-shé

Adroit, wap-sor.

Adversary, i-lam-twr

Affection, a-ta-wit

Affectionate, a-ta-witla

Affirm, *to,* c-a-kw-sha

After, é-rw-é-sra

Afternoon, pa-kwk-an-mai-é-rw-é

Afterwards, a-na-cha-ré

Again, a-na-cha-ré

Age, pwi, an-nw-im.

Agreeable, shir

Ah ! alalá, atei

Alarm, *an,* tí-tar-shi-tla

Aliment, t-kwa-tat

Alone, ksa *added to personal pron.* ink-sa, *I alone;* im-ksa, *thou alone.*

All, klar

Along, *to run,* kat-nem-akw-sha, shana, t, k, tarnei

Also, kws-ré

Although, kla-pré, n-chi-ké

Always, kwa-lis-sim

Amass, *to,* na-ki-wi-sha, wia, ta, k, tarnei

Among, pa, *at the end of the word*

Amount. *That amounts to nothing,* aw-ti-ka, at-shi-na

Amputate, *to,* sar-kle-sha, ka, ta, kom, tarnei

Amuse, *to, one's self,* an-we-i-sha, shana, ta, k, tarnei, lep-swissa, wɪa, wɪta, wɪk, tarneɪ, skré-wisha, wɪa, wɪta, ɪk, tarneɪ

Ancestors, n-chɪ-n-chɪ-ma
Ancient, mɪ-ma
And, w-ɪ-na
Anger, lɪ-wa-tɪt, chɪ-la-kwɪt
Animal, ka-kɪ-a
Announce, *to*, ta-mwn-sha, shana, ta, nenk, tarneɪ, ta-lw-ak-sa, aska, askta, aɪsk, tarneɪ
Annoy, *to*, a-na-nwɪ-a-kw-sha, la, ta, k, tarneɪ
Ant, sklw-eɪ-sa
Antlers, ɪ-w-kas
Anus, skras
Appetite, a-na-wit
Applaud, *to*, e-a-kw-sha
Apprehensive, wɪé-chw-tla, skaw-tla
Approach, *to*, wɪ-na-no-sha, na, ta, k, tarneɪ
Arid, rɪ-a-o
Arm, (*weapon*,) tw-ɪm-pas
Arm, (*limb*,) ópap
Armor, (*cuirass*) krem-na-was
Arrive, *to*, wɪ-a-na-wɪ-sha, a, ta, m, tarneɪ
Arrow, ka-ɪ-a-so
Artery, a-kw-sha-kws
As, a-na-kws
Ashamed, pɪ-na-klw-ɪ-a-tla, *to be ashamed*, pɪ-na-klw-ɪ-a-sha, na, ta, k, tarneɪ
Aspen, nɪ-nɪ
Ass, *an*, ɪ-a-mash-kwssɪ
Assassin, pa-pɪn-shé, sa-ta-wɪ
Attach, *to*, wa-la-krɪc-sha, ka, ta, kom, tarneɪ, enkast-sha, ka, ta, kom, tarneɪ, *to become attached to*, pɪna-wala-krɪc-sha, pɪna-en-kast-sha
Attachment, wa-la-krɪc-ka-was, enkast-ka-was
Auditor, am-sɪ-a-rw-a-tla

Augment, *to*, lar-tra-na-sha, na, ta, k, tarneɪ Maɪ *is sometimes put before* lar
Aunt, parar
Autumn, tɪ-am.
Avarice, tw-at-sa-ré-wɪt
Avaricious, tw-at-sa-ré
Avow, ta-ma-peɪsk-sha, a, ta, om, tarneɪ
Avowal, ta-ma-peɪshkt
Awake, *to*, tar-shɪk-sha, a, ta, k, tarneɪ
Awl, stɪ.
Axe, kro-ɪs-kan, wat-sok

B.

Babbler, *a*, na-twn-tla, es-senw-ɪ-tla
Back, *the*, kop-kop, sɪ-wɪ
Bad, ché-lw-ɪt, chaw-ow, mel-la.
Bag, tatash
Bagatelle, *a*, pa-twn
Bait, ta-kwk-twk-tesh
Bake, *to*, ta-mak-sha, a, ta, &c
Ball, ta-nɪns, ɪ-el-pas, ɪ-la-pat
Bank *of a river*, a-leɪ
Baptize, *to*, pe-tla-sha, na, ta, tk, tarneɪ
Baptism, pé-tlat
Barge, n-chɪ-wasses, pot
Bark, psa
Barrel, ta-mo-lɪsh
Barrier, kra-lar
Basket, ta-ta-she
Bathe, *to*, wɪ-na-né-sha, na, ta, k, tarneɪ
Be, *to*, wa, wat-sha, wata, tarneɪ, *I am*, ɪnk-nesh-wa
Beads, ké-pet
Beak, nws-no
Bear, (*she*) *a*, tw-i-tash, a-na-wɪ, ɪ-a-ka

Bear, to, (bring forth), ırısha, ırıa, ırıta, ırık, tarneı

Beard, shw-o

Bearded, shw-o-ié

Beat, to, tı-wı-sha, a, ta, k, tarneı, to get beat, pına-shapa-tı-wa-sha

Beautiful, shır

Beaver, ı-ra, wınsh-pwsh

Because, kwn-kın

Bed, pé-no-pa-ma

Bedbug, tı-wa-lı

Bee, wı-twı-nat

Before, wa-twı, sra, (adv of time) wa-twı, Acc and Dat wa-twı-chen

Beginning, w-ıt

Beggar, ı-er-tı-tla

Behind, a-nak, Gen a-nak-che-nık, Acc and Dat anak-chen.

Believe, prw-ı-sha, na, ta, k, tarneı

Bell, wı-na-cha-tla, kwa-lal-kwa-lal

Belly, na-wet, nwt

Below, mı-tı, ra-lok, Gen ra-lok-ché-nık

Belt, wa-la-krı-ka-was, wa-la-chw-ıks

Bench, a-y-ka-was

Benign, l-rat-tem-na

Besides, a-na-cha-ré

Bet, to, a-l-o-sha, na, ta, k, tarneı

Better, ma-ı-shır.

Beyond, kw-nınk.

Bile, ma-resh

Bind, to, wa-la-krık-sha, en-kastk-sha

Birds, the, ka-kı-a-ma

Biscuit, sa-phl

Bite, to, chem-sha, shana, ta, k, tarneı

Black, sh-mwk

Blacken, to, sh-mwk-a-kw-sha, ıa, ta, k, tarneı

Bladder, e-ws-pa-ma

Blame, to, ne-te-no-sha, na, ta, k, tarneı

Blanket, wt-pas, sha-tcı, *white blanket*, p-la-she, pı-et

Blind, wam-nam-sha, shı-shı-ws

Blood, tı-nı-wı-né, é-lwk, *to stain with blood*, tı-nı-woın-sha, a, ta, k, tarneı *Blood stained*, tı-nı-woın-ıe

Blossom, to, wa-pok-sha, na-tı-sha

Blow, to, sa-pw-lık-sha, a, ta, om, tarneı

Blue, lô-ınet

Boat, n-chı-wasses, pot.

Body, wa-o-nok-shes

Boil, to, (act) tw-a-sha-sha, na, ta, k, tarneı, (neut) e-mw-lat-sha, na, ta, tk, tarneı

Bole, twk-saı, twk-saı

Bond, na-kwn, m-na-kwn.

Bone, pıp-she

Bonnet, takmal

Book, tı-mash

Booty, w-sha-nıkt

Born, *to be*, wa-krısh-tra-na-sha, wat-sha, shana, ta

Bosom, nı

Boucan, *to, meat*, paı-na-te-sha, shana, ta, k, tarneı

Bow, tw-ımpas

Bowel, *large*, ark-pash, *small*, pı-pı

Box, *a*, wa-kram

Boy, a-sw-an, tar-nwt-shwnt

Bracelet, a-lel

Branch, *large*, pa-tısh, *small*, kra-ta-lıl.

Brave, wıe-chw-nal, as-kaw-nal, le-kok-nal

Bread, sa-plıl, *camash bread*, a-la-ıs

Break, *to*, r-klak-wı-na-sha, na, ta, k, tarneı *to break a horse*, wa-sha-twı-sha, a, ta, k, tarneı

Breast, nı, *the breasts*, ne-krot

Breath, lı-a-shw-ıt

Breathe, *to*, ı-a-sha, a-ash-na, ta, nık, tarneı

Bridle, sa-pat-sam-pa-was

Brigand, sa-ta-wı, kwa-alı, chı-a-w-ow

Brilliant, lor

Bring, *to*, na-na-shamsh, ma, mta, m, tarneı

Broth, tw-a-ert

Brother, *elder*, pı-ap, ı-a-ıa, na-ı-a-ıas, *younger* (*named by the elder*), srop, (*by the sister*), patsht, (*by both*), ne-ka, kwk-son, ın-kaks

Brother-in-law, mı-ow

Brown, lam-t-lam-t

Bud, ı́-kw-alm, trıl-rıt

Build, *to*, nıt-anı-sha, a, ta, k, tarneı

Burn, *to*, élw-sha, na, ta, kom, tarneı

Burning, ó-lw-tla

Burthen, shap-she

Business, ta-kwn

Bustard, ha-kak

Busy, *to be*, ta-kwn-ı-sha, ta-kwn-ıa, ıta, ık, tarneı.

Butter, ı-a-pash

Butterfly, wa-lor-wa-lar

Button, par-pa-was

Button, *to*, par-kr-p-sha, na, ta, wm, tarneı

Buy, *to*, ta-nıı-a-sha, shana, ta-mıata, tamıak, tarneı

By, kı, pa

C.

Cabin, nıt

Cache, *a*, nıt-she

Cache, *to*, sha-pa-l-kw-ık-sha, shana, ta, k, tarneı

Calm, pesht

Calumniator, ın-mo-tla

Calumny, ın-mot

Calvary, Calvaıre

Camp, wa-w-twk-pa-ma, *winter camp*, a-no-tash, *spring camp*, sha-tesh, *to break up the camp*, w-sha-na-sha, na, ta, k, tarneı, *from the plain on the bank of the river*, ws-ta-mık-sha, *on the banks up the river*, ws-tw-nık-sha, *on the banks of the river off in the plain*, ws-pı-wk-sha

Candle, la-ker-rı-ta-was

Canoe, w-as-scs

Canoe pole, e-ı-ash

Capable, rı́-to, wap-sor

Capsule, sra-o-kas

Carbine, krat-ka-tı, tw-ım-pas.

Carcass, pıp-she

Carnage, n-chı-pı-at-nat, n-chı-pı-klı-a-wıt

Carp, rwn

Carry, *carry away, to*, na-na-sha, na, ta, k, tarneı, *to carry on the back*, shap-sha, a, ta, k, tarneı, *any one on the back*, ka-lak-sha, a, ta, k, tarneı

Cascades, kop

Cask, ta-mw-lıtsh

Cat, pısh-pısh, pwsh

Catechise, *to*, sap-sw-kwa-sha, na, ta, nem, tarneı

Catechism, sap-sw-kwat

Caterpillar, sc-ı-sc-ı

Cease, *to, for a moment*, tra-w-ser-sa, na, ta, k, tarneí, *for ever*, w-ser-sa, na, ta, k, tarneı

Cedar, nan-k

Cellar, r-nem-nı
Cemetery, ı-aw-a-ta-sha, l-cha-cha
Centre, pa-kwk, pa-chw
Certain, nw-ıt-ka, kw-ı-am
Chain, to, wa-la-krık-sha, a, ta, kom, tarneı
Chair, a-ı-ka-was, a-ık-pa-ma, a-ı-kws
Chapel, ta-la-pw-sha-pa-ma-nıt
Charcoal, la-pw-ık, la-kro-she
Charitable, sh-nw-eı-tla
Chaste, wa-ta-twı-al
Chat, to, na-twn-sha, na, ta, k, tarneı, es-sé-nw-ıs-sa, ıa, ıta, k, tarneı
Cheek, té-pesh
Cherish, to, a-ta-wı-sha, a, ta, k, tarneı, a-tem-na-sha, na, ta, k, tarneı, at-ker-sha, na, ta, ker, tarneı
Cherry, té-mesh
Chief, a, mı-a-war, mı-or
Child, a, a-sw-an, pl mı-a-nash-ma, little child, pw-a-she
Childbed, ı-rı-te
Chimney, wı-la-ta-was, é-lwks-pa-ma
Chin, té-nen
Chisel, raps-raps-tlı
Christian, pé-tla-mı
Church, tana-mw-twmpamanıt
Cicatrix, pa-ı-w-ıt
Clean, kı-ak, kw-ır
Clear, kra ır
Climb, to, a mountain, pa-na-tı-sha, a, ta, k, tarneı, a tree, at-ke-nı-sha, a, ta, k, tarneı
Close, to, kra-la-ré-sha, ıa, ta, ık, tarneı
Cloud, shw-a-tash
Coal, live, la-kra-wksh
Coat, tat-pas
Cock, Le-coq

Cold, kré-set, ké-pes
Cold, a, k-krw-ıt, ta-no-rat, to have a cold, k-krwı-sha, a, ta, n, tarneı
Colt, kra-ık-kws-sı
Comb, tw-em-pas
Combat, pa-tı-wıt, pı-at-nat, pı-klı-a-wıt
Combat, to, pı-at-na-sha, na, ta, k, tarneı, pı-klı-a-wı-sha, a, ta, k, tarneı
Come, to, wı-na-shansh, ma, mta, m, tarneı
Command, to, ta-ma-nwı-sha, a, ta, k, tarneı
Commencement, w-ıt
Compassionate, to, sh-nw-eı-sha, a, ta, k, tarneı
Compassionate, adj sh-nw-eı-tla
Conduct, to, a-nıt-shata-sha, na, ta, k, tarneı
Confess, to, pı-na-ta-ma-peık-sha, na, ta, k, tarneı
Conquer, l-rat a-nı-sha, a, ta, k, tarneı
Construct, to, a-nı-sha, a, ta, k, tarneı
Consult, to, sap-nı-sha, ıa, ta, k, tarneı
Contented, kwa-tla-nı
Contradict, to, ta-na-war-sha, na, ta, k, tarneı
Contrition, tem-na-n-mı, nar-tıt
Converse, to, na-twn-sha, na, ta, k, tarneı, es-se-nw-ıs-sa, ıa, ıta, k, taıneı
Cook, to, a-tı-sha, a, ta, k, tarneı, under the ashes, w-sha-nak-sha, a, ta, k, tarneı
Cooked, a-tı-she
Copper, ma-ral-n-mı
Cord, ta-rwr

Corpse, l-cha-cha, at-na-nı
Corrupt, to, sı-sw-sa, na, ta, k, tarneı
Cotton, sıl
Cough, k-krwt
Cough, to, ke-krwı-sha, a, ta, k, tarneı
Counsel, tw-ım-wt ,
Counsel, to, tw-mı-w-sha, na, ta, k, tarneı, sha-pa-prw-ı-sha, ıa, ta, k, tarneı
Count, to, tı-ta-ma-sha, na, ta, k, tarneı
Country, tet-sham
Courage, r-to-tem-na
Courageous, n-chı-tem-na, wı-ć-chw-nal
Course, paw-la-wert
Cover, war-kw-aw-ka-was
Cover, to, ka-maı-a-kw-sha, ıa, ta, k, tarneı, shapa-she-ınk-sha, a, ta, k, tarneı
Cow, mws-mw-sın, a-ı-et-wks
Cowardly, wı-ć-chw-tla, a-skaw-tla
Crab, kas-tı-la
Creator, a-nı-tla
Crime, chó-lwı-tıt, mella-wıt
Cross, wa-wt-sa-ké, wa-ta-plı-é
Cross, to, ı-a-ro-ık-sha, a, ta, k, tarneı
Crow, a, ro-ro
Crown, wa-la-loks
Cruel, sa-ta-wı, chó-lw-ıt, mella
Crupper, tw-ın-pa-ma
Cultıvate, ta-ma-nık-sha, a, ta, k, tarneı
Curıous, sı-ak-tw-ı-tla
Curıous, to be, sı-ak-tw-ı-sha, a, ta, k, tarneı
Custom, tra-nat
Cut, to, sar-klek-sha, ka, ta, kom, tarneı , to cut wood, sar-kl-cha

D.

Dagger, ra-pıls-mı
Dance, to, wa-sha-sha, na, ta, k, tarneı
Dart, ta-no
Dart, to, p-tı-a-sha, na, ta, k, tarneı
Daughter-ın-law, p-nash
Day, ra-ır
Deaf, to-lak-met-sı-w
Dear, a-taw
Death, at-nat, klı-a-wıt
Decamp, to, w-sha-ua-sha, na, ta, k, tarneı
Delırıum, pa-leı-wıt
Delude, to, (in order to take) tam-klw-er-wı-sha, a, ta, &c
Demon, che-lw-ıt-wap-sor, mel-la-wap-sor
Descend, to, a-ık-sha, ka, ta, k, tarneı
Desert, to, wı-na-nın-sha, a, ta, k, tarneı
Design, without, a-w-tı-ka, a-chı-na, kw-la-lı
Desire, to, lwk-lw-krwa-sha, na, ta, k, tarneı
Die, to, at-na-sha, na, t, k, tarneı, dying, shı-wct, ı-a-noaı, at-na-ta-ta
Difficult, o-ı
Dıg, to, re-nem-sha, na, ta, k, tarneı
Dirty, che-mak
Disband, to, pa-pa-wı-a-pa-sha, na, ta, nk, tarneı
Disdain, to, chó-ı-sha, na, ta, k, tarneı
Dish, tı-kaı
Disobey, kré-shem-sha, na, ta, k, tarneı
Do, akw-sha, anısha
Dog, kwssı-kwssı

Dollar, tá-lä
Door, wes-pas
Drag, *one's self*, sa-pro-na-ti-sha, a, ta, k, tarnei
Draw, *to*, kré-up-sha, na, ta, nk, tarnei
Dress, *to*, *(a skin)* pae-la-me-rek-sha, a, ta, k, tarnei
Dress, *to*, *(one's self)* tat-pas-issa, ia, ita, ik, tarnei
Dressed, tat-pas-ie
Drink. *to*, ché-sha, na, ta, k, tarnei
Drive, *to*, *before one*, i-w-sha, na, ta, k, awi-wk, tarnei
Drown, *to*, i-a-o-wei-kla-mei-sha, ka, ta, k, tarnei
Drowsy, *to grow*, pé-nw-a-ta-sha, na, ta, k, tarnei
Drum, kwi-kwi-las
Drunkard, pa-lei-tlalom-ki, ta-war-ki, tor-ki
Dry, ri-a-o
Dry, *to*, la-ri-a-wi-sha, a, ta, k, tarnei
Duck, rat-rat, wish-twk
Dull, a-i-a-iash
Dung, pé-shet
During, pa, *at the end of the word*, a-na-ko

E.

Ear, met-si-w
Earth, tet-sham
Easy, teer, chaw-e-tok
Eat, *to*, t-kwa-ta-sha, na, ta, k, tarnei, *to eat on the road*, la-se-la-si-sa, a, ta, k, tarnei, *to eat before starting*, wé-mé-tep-sa, a, ta, k, tarnei, *to eat at the camp*, trask-sa, ka, ta, k, tarnei
Egg sw-si-lo, ta-mam

Eight, pa-ra-tw-mat, wi-mé-tat
Eighty, pa-ra-tw-ma-tep-tit
Elder, *(tree)*, m-ta-pa-whw
Elder, *the elder*, wat-wima, ia-ia-ma, *elder brother*, pi-ap, *elder sister*, pat
Embark, *to*, wa-sha-sha, na, ta, k, tarnei
Employ, *to*, sha-pa-kwt-kw-sha, ia, ta, k tarnei
Empty, ta-ler
Empty, *to*, ta-ler-a-kw-sha
Encamp, wa-w-twk-sha, a, ta, k, tarnei
Enclosure, kra-lar
End *(of a thing)*, la-krit
Enemy, tw-al-ra
Engraving, ti-mash
Enlighten, *to*, la-krai-ri-sha, a, ta, k, tarnei
Ennui, a-na-nwi-wit
Enough, aw-kwel
Enter, *to*, a-sha, shana, a-shta, a-shen, tarnei
Entire, na-men, na-mel
Envy, pi-na-kai-wa-wit
Envy, *to*, pi-na-kai-wa-sha, na, ta, k, tarnei
Equal, kwal-re, kws-re, kwks-sini
Esteem, *to*, a-shir-sha
Everywhere, kler-pein
Evil, ché-lw-i tit, mel-la-wit
Exchange, *to*, tre-ta-mi-a sha, na, ta, k, tarnei
Excrement, pé-shet
Expect, *to*, pa-pa-wa-krict-sha, *(wait)*
Expire, *to*, at-na-sha, na, ta, k, tarnei
Extend, *to*, aws-nik-sha, a, ta, k, tarnei
Eye, a-ches, *pl* at-ches
Eye-brow, sle-mo-pop

F.

Fable, wa-tısh, wa-tı-tash-nmı-tamo, *to tell fables*, wa-tı-sha, a, ta, k, tarneı

Face, té-pesh

Faint, *to, with hunger*, a-na-we-ık-sha, ka, ta, k, tarneı, (*otherwise*), la-weı-at-na-sha na, ta, k, tarneı

Fall, t-kra-w-krıt

Fall, *to*, t-kra-w-krı-sha, a, ta, k, tarneı, tré-tam-ché-nwı-sha, a, ta, k, tarneı, *to fall as grain does*, trap-sa-wı-sa, a, ta, k, tarneı

False, tshesk, tsheskwıt, tshent-la

Far, *very far*, w-ı-et

Fast, *a*, t-kwa-tesh

Fast, *to*, chaw-t-kwa-ta-sha, na, ta, k, tarneı

Fat, chrao

Father, p-sheut, p-shut

Father-in-law, p-shes

Fault, ché-lw-ı-tıt

Fear, wıe-chw-ıt, skaw-ıt, le-kok-wıt

Fear, *to*, wı-é-chw-sha, na, ta, n-k, tarneı, as-kaw-ssa, na, ta, n-mk, tarneı, le-kok-sha, na, nmk, tarneı

Feather, wap-tas

Feeble, lk-kap, sha-law

Feign, *to*, chesk-sha, a, ta, k, tarneı

Fell, *to*, warckl-cha, ka, ta, kom, tarneı

Female, a-ı-et-wk

Fence, kra-lar

Fever, la-rw-ır

Fever and ague, chw-eı-tla

Field, ta-ma-nı-che

Fifteen, pw-tempt (*ten*) w-ı-na (*and*) pa-rat (*five*)

Fifty, pa-rap-tıt

Fight, *to*, (*quarrel*), pa-pa-tı-wa-sha, (*in battle*), pı-at-na-sha, na, ta, k, tarneı, pı-klı-a-wı-sha, a, ta, k, tarneı

File, *o*, sa-pat-sam-ka-was

Fill, *to*, ke-kwm-a-kw-sha, ıa, ta, k, tarneı

Find, *to*, ı-er-sha, na, ta, n-k, tarneı

Finder, *a*, ı-er-tla

Finger, é-pap

Finish, *to*, na-krı-sha, na, ta, k, tarneı

Fire, é-lwks, *to set on fire*, tansk-sha, ka, ta, an, tarneı

First, wa-twı, rw-she, *at the end of the pers pron*

Fish, t-kwı-na-tıt, nw-sor

Fish, *to*, (*with a net*), kwı-kwı-sha, a, ta, k, tarneı, (*with a line*), ner-tı-sha, a, ta, k, tarneı

Fishing pole, tı-raı

Fish hook, krı-a-chı

Five, pa-rat, *five persons*, par-na-o

Flag, cha-wa-ı-lok

Flame, ı-la-wı-a-ta

Flask, é-nen

Flat, tı-kaı

Flea, ash-nam

Flee, *to*, wı-na-nın-sha

Flesh, né-kw-et

Flour, sa-phıl-twt-nı

Flow, *to*, wa-na-sha, na, ta, k, tarneı

Flower, na-tıt

Flower, *to*, na-tı-sha, a, ta, k, tarneı

Flute, pı-w-ten

Fly, mwr-lı

Fly, *to*, *away*, wo-ı-na-sha, na, ta, k, tarneı

Foal, *to*, rı-sha, a, ta, k, tarnei

Follow, to, twa-na-sha, na, ta, k, tarnei
Foolish, pa-lei, to talk foolishly, pa-lei-sha
Foot, w-ra, on foot, wi-na-ni, w-ra-kilk
Foot-print, wa-tik-she
For, ka-o, for me, n-mi-ei, n-mi-ka-iei, for thee, e-mi-ka-iei for him, pen-mi-ka-iei, for us, ne-é-mi-ka-iei. for you, é-ma-mi-ka-iei, for them, pe-mi-ka-iei
Force, r-t-tw-it, kol-tep-wit
Forehead, shw-a
Forget, to, lak-sha, na, ta, k, tarnei
Fork, pa-kro-ka-was
Formerly, ini-wi, mi-mi
Fornicate, to, wa-ta-twi-sha, a, ta k, tarnei
Fornication, wa-ta-tw-it
Fornicator, wa-ta-twi-tla
Fortune, ta-nw-et
Forty, pi-nep-tit
Fountain, nwm
Four, pi-nept, speaking of persons, pi-na-po
Fox, red, lwt-sa, grey, té-li-pa
Freeze, to, (geler), shé-sha-sha, na, ta, k, tarnei, (glacer), ta-ka-ok-sha, a, ta, k, tarnei
Fresh, petl-ro
Friday, par-na-mi-pa, pa-ra-ti-pa
Friend, rai, shisk-twa
Frighten, to, sha-pa-wi-ei-chw-sha, sha-pa-skaw-ssa, to be frightened at, pi-na-wi-ei-chw-sha
Frog, a-lw-krat-a-lw-krat
Froth, pw-shem
Fruit, ta-ma-nikt
Full, ke-mim, ke-kwn

G.

Gain, i-she
Gain, to, i-sha, i-shna, i-shta, ishtk, tarnei
Game, ka-kia, to hunt game, mis-tei-wa-sha
Game, a, a-nw-aét, skré-wit, lep-swit
Game bag, kla-kam
Gape, to, ta-or-sha, na, ta, k, tarnei
Garden, ta-ma-wit-she
Gather, to, fruit, te-ma-ni-sha, ia, ta, k, tarnei
Gay, kwa-tla-ni, ti-a-ni
Gently, tlw-ei
Gift, ni-she, ni-tw-it
Girl, pte-wiks, unmarred, te-mai
Girth, na-wat-pa-ma
Give, to, a-ni-sha, a, ta, k, tarnei, ni-tw-i-sha, a, ta, k, tarnei
Glass, a, pi-na-krć-nw-ta-was-mni twk-sai, klas
Glass, krć-nw-ta-was
Glove, lw-kwm
Gnat, wa-wa
Go, to, wi-na-sha, nana, ta, k, tarnei, aw-namtk-atsha, let us go, to go for one, wi-na-no-sha, na, ta, k, tarnei, wiana-wi-no-sha, shana, ta, ik, tarnei, wa-ses-ki, to go at large, pi-wt-sha, shana, ta, to go out, at-sha, a, ta, k, tarnei, to go in a canoe, wa-ses-ki, w-sha-na-tesha, shana, ta, ik, tarnei
Goblet, che-ta-ta-was, twk-sai-kwk-sai
Gold, tá-la
Good, shir
Goose, wa-nep-tas
Gooseberry, ré-nen
Grace, roe-mi-pa-ma-ni-she

Grain, ta-ma-nıkt
Grandfather, tı-la
Grandmother, katla
Grant, a-nı-sha, anıa, anıta, anık, tarneı
Grass, was-ko, sek-sek
Gratis, a-w-tı-ka, at-shı-na
Gray, la-met, kash-kash, pa-pre
Grease, ı-a-pash
Great, n-chı
Greedy, kr-nep-né
Green, lô-met
Grind, to, twt-sha, na, ta, k, tarneı
Grow, to, ta-war-sha, na, ta, k, tarneı
Grumbler, thk
Guide, wı-a-tweı
Guide, to, tw-a-na-sha, na, ta, k, tarneı
Gum, ısh-ré
Gummy, ısh-reı
Gun, tw-ım-pas

H.

Ha, a-teı
Habit, tra-nat, w-sha-ı-kwıt
Hail, kw-ı-kw-ı
Hail, to, kw-ı-kw-ı-sha, a, ta, k, tarneı
Hair, lao-lao
Hand, é-pap
Handkerchief, tkweı-weı-wısh, tws-mors
Handle, of a basket, pot, &c, waneptas
Hang, to, chaw-kré-sha, ka, ta, k, tarneı, to hang one's self, pına before the verb
Happiness, shır-w-ıt
Harangue, to, na-te-no-sha, na, ta, k, tarneı

Hard, klw-eı
Hare, wı-la-lık
Hasten, to, ké-to-as-kw-sha, ıa, ta, k, tarneı
Hat, (man's) tak-mal, (woman's) sa-rı-lı
Hatch, to, ra-ta-tw-a, na-ta-ık-ta, k, tarneı
Hate, to, shı-wet-no-sha, ché-ı-sha
Have, to, a-wa-wat-sha, wata, wak, tarneı, I have, nesh-wa or wash-nesh
Hawk, krıa
Hay, shw-ıs
He, pe-nk, pl p-mak
Head, klam-tor, tel-pı
Headstrong, kre-shem-tla
Hear, to, met-sı-a-rw-a-sha, na, ta, k, tarneı
Heart, tem-na
Heat, é-ı-chw
Heaven, roe-mı-pa-ma-tıt-sham
Heavenly, roe-ım-pa-ma
Heavy, ko
Hell, mı-tı-chen, en-per
Hemp, ta-rws
Hen, le-kok
Henceforth, chı-né-nınk
Herd, ta-no
Here, ıt-chı-na, acc and dat ıt-chen
Hide, kla-meı-ık-sha, a, ta, k, tarneı
High, rœmı
Hill, pwsh-teı
Hind, ıapnıt
His, pen-mınk
Hogshead, ta-mw-lıtsch
Hole, t-krw-aıt
Homicide, sa-ta-wı, pa-pınsh
Horn, en-nen
Horrible, che-lw-ıt

Horse, kwssi, *race horse*, sha-pa-la-wei-pa-ina
Horseman, wa-sha-tla
House, nit, *at the house of*, pa *at the end of the word or* n-mi-pa
How, mish-nin, mani
How much, *how many*, mélt
Humid, i-a-kle-pit
Hummingbird, r-mem-sa
Humpbacked, ma-kar-né
Hundred, pw-tap-tit
Hunger, a-na-wit
Hungry, *to be*, a-na-wi-sha, a, ta, k, tarnei
Hunt, *to*, w-sa-la-tis-sa, ia, ta, k, tarnei
Husband, am
Hypocrite, chesk-tla

I.

I, nk, nes, nesh
Ice, tor, ta-ka-ok
Idea, prw-i
If, pa-ish
Ignorant, pa-lei, *to be ignorant*, chaw-a-shw-kwa-sha, na, ta, k, tarnei
Imbecile, pa-lei, a-i-a-iash
Importune, *to*, a-na-nwi-a-kw-sha, ia, ta, k, tarnei
Impossible, taw-na-wa-tesk
Impure, wa-ta-tw-i-tla
In, pa *at the end of the word*
Inclose, *to*, kra-la-ré-sha, in, ta, ik, tarnei
Incorrigible, kré-shem-tla
Indian, ten, na-ti-tait
Infirm, pa-i-w-ié
Inhabitant, ten, na-ti-tait
Insolent, ta-ma-kal
Instant, sat-i-kws

Instruct, *to*, sap-sw-kwa-sha, na, ta, k, tarnei
Insult, *to*, w-re-tem-sha, na, ta, nk, tarnei, wa-w-kr-sha, ka
Insulting, w-re-tem-tla
Intelligent, wap-sor
Interpret, *to*, ta-ma-sw-ik-sha, a, ta, k, tarnei
Interpreter, ta-ma-sw-ik-tla
Interrogate, *to*, sap-ni-sha, a, ta, k, tarnei
Intestine, *an*, ark-pash
Intimidate, *to*, sha-pa-wi-é-chw-sha, na, ta, nemk, tarnei
Intoxicate, *to*, sha-pa-pa-lei-sha, na, ta, k, tarnei
Intrepid, wi-é-chw-nal, as-kaw-nal
Inundate, *to*, i-a-o-wei-na-sha, na, ta, k, tarnei
Inundation, i-a-o-wei-nat
Invincible, kwa-la-lé
Invisible, chaw-tei-kré-nw-tash
Iron, sti, ra-ra-i-wk
Irritate, *to*, sha-pa-li-wa-ti-sha, a, ta, k, tarnei, *to become irritated*, is-ser-sa, na, ta, nk, tarnei
Island, é-ma, ma-wi

J.

Jaw, em
Jay, ai-ai
Jealous, pa-ler-tla
Joy, kwa-tlat
Judge, *to*, na-te-no-sha, na, ta, k, tarnei
Judgment, na-te-not
Juggle, *to*, lar-pi-sha, a, ta, k, tarnei
Juggler, tw-a-ti

K.

Keep, *to*, nak-no-ı-sha, a, ta, k, tarneı
Kernel, tem-la-tem-la
Kettle, twk-saı
Key, wa-rel-pa-was
Kick, *to*, pa-ta-na-wı-na-sha, na, ta, k, tarneı
Kill, *to*, pı-at-na-sha, na, ta, k, tarneı, pı-klı-a-wī-sha, ıa, ta, k, tarneı
Kindle, *to*, e-lwk-sha, shana, ta, k, tarneı
King, mı-a-war, mı-or
Kiss, por-sa
Kneel, *to*, op-te-na-ık-sha, aıka, aıkta, ık, tarneı
Knife, ra-pıls-mı, krwt-krwt-lı
Knot, *to*, wa-la-krık-sha, en-kast-sha
Know, *to*, a-shw-kwa-sha, na, ta, k, tarneı, shw-kwa-nı-sha, teksha, shaua, ta, om, te-ka-nı-sha, ıa, ta, k, tarneı

L.

Lace, *to*, ta-mas-k-sha, ka, ta, am, tarneı.
Ladder, wa-tı-ka-tla
Lake, wa-tam
Lame, kar-nı
Lamprey, a-swm, ka-sw-ıas
Land, *to*, a-leı-sha, shana, ta, ak, tarneı
Language, na-twn, es-sé-aw-ıt
Large, n-chı
Lark, rol-rol
Last, la-kré-sa-tla, n-nak
Laugh, *to*, tı-a-sha, na, ta, k, tarneı, *we do not laugh*, chaw-tes-tı-a-sha, *to laugh at*, sa-pé-lem-sa, na, ta, k, tarneı

Law, ta-ma-nw-ıt
Lazy, e-tok-tla
Lead, *to*, na-na-sha, na, ta, k, tarneı, *to lead a horse*, tı-men-ta-tı-sha, n, ta, k, tarneı
Leaf, apr-apr
Lean, kra-ıo
Leap, t-lwp
Leap, *to*, tlwp-sha, na, ta, k, tarneı
Learned, wap-sor
Leather, 6-par
Leave, *to*, w-ré-sha, na, ta, k, tarneı, wıa-nok-sha
Leech, l-kop-sha
Leg, w-ra
Lend, *to*, w-emp-shı-sha, a, ta, k, tarneı
Lengthen, *to*, at-shar-to-sha, shana, ta, newk, tarneı
Less, ma-ı-ka-ı-wa, maı-mé-la
Letter, tı-mash
Liar, chesk-tla
Lick, *to*, mé-laı-mé-laı-nra, na, ta, k, tarneı
Lie, *to*, chesk-sha, na, ta, k, tarneı
Lie, *to, down*, pı-na-o-ré-sha, na, ta, nk, tarneı, mam-rw-ı-sha, na, ta, k, tarneı
Life, wa-krısh-wıt
Light, *adj* por
Light, *a*, la-ka ır-rı-ta-was, ra-ır
Light, *to, a pipe*, wa-lok-sha, shana, ta, k, tarneı
Like, kws-ré
Linen, ta-rws-mı
Lip, em
Listen, *to*, met-sı-a-rw-a-sha, na, ta k, tarneı, a-ın-sha, na, ta, k, tarneı
Little, ık-sıks, wap-taı, ık-kes, ı-kat-ı-kat

Little, *a*, ık-kés, mé-la
Liver, ma-kresh
Living, wa-krish
Load, *to*, shapa-shap-sha, a, ta, k, tarneı, *a load*, shap-she
Loan, w-emp-shıt
Lodge, nıt
Long, kat-nam
Lose, w-ré-sha, na, ta, k, tarneı
Louse, (*of head,*) a-pen, (*of body,*) pa-w-lwk
Love, a-ta-wıt
Love, *to*, at-ker-sha, na, ta, ker, tarneı, tem-na-sha, nana, ta, nak, tarneı Speaking of little children and animals they say, nem-no-sha, *aimer des yeux*, at-shes-wı-sha, wıa, ta, ık, tarneı, *to have an affection for*, a-ta-wisha, ata-wıa, ıta, ık, tarneı
Low, mıtı, *low people*, o-lım-ten, s-lım-na-tı-ta-ıt, o-lım-pas-ton
Lung, shw-shop

M.

Mad, pa-leı
Magpie, aı-aı
Maize, stwrs-wa-kwl
Man, wınsh, ten, na-tı-taıt, *men*, ten-ma, na-tı-taıt-ma, wınshmıa
Mane, to-ta-nık
Manner, tra-nat
Many, lar, lır, r-lak, pa-la-leı
Mare, aı-et-ws-kws-sé
Mark, tı-mash
Mark, *to*, tı-ma-sha, na, ta, k, tarneı
Marrow, ta-po
Master, kw-tlı
Mat, skw-as, ont-ko, klım
Matches, tw-nıs

Me, ınk, ın
Meadow, (*on the mountains*) tak, (*in the plains*) é-ı-par
Measure, *to*, tı-ta-ma-sha, na, ta, k, tarneı
Medal, weı-wısh
Medecine, plar, (*Indian jugglery*) ta-o-tı-nwk
Medecineman, tw-a-tı
Meet, *to*, ws-ta-mı-a-sha, na, ta, k, tarneı
Middle, pa-kwk, pa-chw
Milk, né-krot
Milk, *to*, sha-pa-wa-na-sha, na, ta, k, tarneı
Mingle, *to*, cı-tw-a-sha, na, ta, k, tarneı
Mint, a-shw-ra-shw-ra
Miserable, chı-a-wo, sh-nw-eı, ı-a-o
Miss, *to, a blow*, wop-taı-sha, a, ta, k, tarneı
Mist, tı-na-ıks, pas-tsat
Moment, sa-tı-kws
Month, al-ıa-ır
Moon, al-raır
Morning, skw-ı-pa
Mother, p-cha
Mother-in-law, p-nash
Mould, sı-sw
Mouldy, *to grow*, sı-swn-ra, a, ta, k, tarneı
Mount, *a horse*, wa-sha-sha, na, ta, k, tarneı
Mountain, pé-tra-nok
Mouse, lı-kas
Mouth, eın, *of a river*, pa-shın-kı-ot
Much, lar, lır, r-lak, pa-la-leı
Mud, mé-kl-kl, *to make a mud wall*, ta-ma-klak-sha, mé-kl-kl-chı
Muddy, mé-kl-kl-ıć
Mule, ı-a-mash-kws-sı
Murder, pı-at-nat, pı-klı-a-wıt

Murderer, pa-pinsh, pi-at-na-tla, pi-kli-a-wi-tla
Music, w-em-pash
Muzzle, nws-no
My, n-mi, en-mi

N.

Nail, (*ongle*) a-sa, (*clou*) wa-kr-pa-was
Naked, aw-nam-ke, ro-yam-ro-yam
Name, wa-nitsh, wa-ni-kw-it
Name, *to,* wa-nik-sha, a, ta, k, tarnei
Named, *to be,* pina *before the verb*
Near, tsi-wes, sa *Gen* sa-ke-nik *Dat* sa-i-a-o *Sa governs the dative except in* sá-en-mi-o, *near me*
Neck, ta-nw-et
Needle, chaw-a-épi
Negro, sh-mwk-ten
Neigh, *to,* i-nem-ra, ma, ta, k, tarnei
Nephew, pitr, pimr
Nerve, w-it-sés
Net, *hand net,* koi-kw, *long net,* t-k-ni
Never, chaw-mwn
New, chem-té
News, ta-ino, ta-lw-askt
Niece, pitr, pimr, pa-i-a
Night, t-sat, *by night,* taw, *before the verb I write by night,* taw-ti-ma-shés
Nine, se-meskt
Ninety, se-mesk-tep-tit
No, chaw, wé-twn
No, (*adj*), chaw-nars, chaw-shin
Nocturnal, t-sat-pa-ma
Noon, pa-kwk-an
Nose, nws-no
Not at all, chaw-me-nan

Nothing, chaw-twn, *that amount to nothing,* a-w-ti-ka, at-shi-na
Now, i-chi-i-kwak, chi-kwk
Number, *to,* ti-ta-ma-sha, na, ta, k, tarnei
Numerous, lar, lir, pa-la-lei, ré-lak
Nurse, *to,* (*suckle*), sha-pa-lw-lwk-sha, ka, ta, lwk, tarnei
Nut, kw-kwsh

O.

Oak, sw-nips
Oar, kro-i-a
Object, ta-kwn, sho-a-chin
Obscure, ta-ham
Obstinate, *to be,* kre-shem-sha, na, ta, k, tarnei
Occupy, kwt-kw-sha, ia, ta, k, tarnei, ra-nei-sha
Odor, ti-wat
Of, n-mi
Oh, a-tei
Oil, wo-litsht
Oil, *to,* wo-lit-shi-sha, a, ta, k, tarnei
Old, *for things,* mi-ma, *for males,* rw-sat, rw-sa-nat, *for females,* tle-ma-ma, *to grow old,* rw-sa-twi-ssa, a, ta, k, tarnei
One, nars, lars, sra
Onion, shak
Open, *to, n* (*as flowers,*) wa-pok-sha, *as an egg,* wa-prk-sha, *act a-*sha-relp-sha, a, ta, k, tarnei
Order, *in order to,* kwn-kin, *or by the gerundive in* tesh, *in order to go to heaven,* rœmitschen winatesh
Order, *an,* ta-ma-nw-it
Order, *to,* ta-ma-nwi-sha, a, ta, k, tarnei
Orphan, a-na-tat

Osier, te-tar-she
Other, te-ner
Our, né-emi, na-ami
Outside of, am-che-nik, *acc and dat* am-chen
Oven, ta-ma-ka-was
Over and above, cha-aw-ka
Overflow, *to*, i-a-o-wei-na-sha
Owl, ha-ha-tla, a-mash, mi-ma-no
Ox, inws-mus, mws-mws-in

P.

Paddle, kro-i-a
Pain, pa-i-w-it
Paint, *to smear one's self with paint*, pi-na-tra-o-i-sha, na, ta, nak, tarnei
Paint, *to*, tra-wi-a-sha, na, ta, k, tarnei, *to paint one's self*, pina *before the verb*
Palisade, em-ma
Pantaloons, sw-la-tas, ni-atsh
Papa, té-ta, to-ta
Paper, ti-mash
Paradise, rœ-mi-pa-ma-tet-sham
Park, kra-lar
Partridge, karno
Passage *of a river*, i-a-ro-ikt, i-a-ro-ik-tesh
Pasture, *to*, spa-ta-sa, na, ta, k, tarnei
Path, i-chet
Paunch, ark-pash
Paw, w-ia
Pay, i-w-sha, i-wsh-na, i-wsh-ta, i-wshk, tarnei
Pea, lć-pois
Pear, chi-cha-i-a, chi-cha
Pearl, ke-pet
Pebble, p-shw-a

Pectoral, ni-pa-ma
Peel, *to*, mi-wk-sha, ka, ta, k, tarnei
Pensive, prw-i-tla
People, ten-ma, na-ti-tait-ma
Perch, 6-lw-kas
Perhaps, kwa-mish, mish-kwak, kwak
Perish, *to*, at-ua-sha, kha-wi-sha
Persevere, twa-na-sha-kwa-lis-sim
Persist, kre-shem-sha.
Person, sha-kwn, sho-a-shin
Pervert, che-lw-it-sha-pa-tra-na-sha, na, ta, k, tarnei
Pheasant, pti
Physician, tok-ter, plar-i-tla
Pickpocket, pa-rw-i-tlam
Picture, ti-mash
Pigeon, me-tal-lo
Pimple, sw-swms
Pin, ka-pws
Pine, ta-pash
Pipe, wi-pai, cha-la-met
Pipe stem, pat-sa-kas
Pistol, ikat-i-kat-tw-im-pas, kui-wa-tw-im-pas
Pity, *to*, shnw-ei-sha, eia, eita, nem, tarnei
Place, n-ma-kwn
Plait, *to*, wa-pa-sha, na, ta, k, tarnei
Plant, *to*, ta-ma-nik-sha, a, ta, k, tarnei
Plate, ti-hai
Play, *to*, a-nw-ei-sna, skrć-wi-sha, lep-swi-sa, a, ta, k, tarnei, *with the hand*, pa-li-o-sha, na, ta, k, tarnei, *with cards*, tam-klak-sha, a, ta, om, tarnei, *to the last penny*, ta-ma-klar-sha, na, ta, k, tarnei
Pledge, a-li-o-she

Pledge, to, a-li-o-sha, na, ta, k, tarnei
Plough, to, shwa-sha-tet-sham
Plumage, wap-tas
Plume, pa-ta-she
Plunder, to, pa-rw-i-sha, na, ta, k, tarnei
Pocket, psa-tes-pas, ta-tws, to put in one's pocket, psa-ta-sa, na, ta, k, tarnei
Pond, wa-tan
Poor, sh-nwei, i-a-o
Pot, twk-sai
Pound, to, twt-sha, na, ta, ak, tarnei
Pour, out, to, i-ar-ta-sha, na, ta, k, tarnei
Powder, la-tor-tor, pors-pors
Powerful, r-t-to, kol-tép
Praise, shir-shw-it
Pray, to, ta-na-mw-twin-sha, na, ta, k, tarnei, ta-la-pw-shak-sha, a, ta, k, tarnei
Prayer, ta-na-mw-twmt, ta-la-pw-sha
Precept, ta-ma-nw-it.
Pregnant, i-ak
Present, a, ni-she, ni-tw-it
Preserve, to, nak-no-i-sha, a, ta, k, tarnei
Pretty, shir
Price, prize, i-w-she
Priest, sh-mwk-tat-pas, le prêtre
Proud, to grow proud, pi-na-chel-sha, na, ta, k, tarnei
Provision, a-pi-she
Purchase, ta-mi-a-she
Pure, wa-ta-twi-al, kw-ir-tem-na
Pursue, tw-a-na-sha, na, ta, k, tarnei

Q.

Quarrel, to, pa-pa-w-ré-tem-sha, na, tu, k, tarnei
Quick, ke-to, cho
Quiver, tw-shes

R.

Rain, tor-tor, sra-wit-it
Rain, to, tor-tor-sha, na, ta, k, tarnei, sra-wi-ti-sha
Rainbow, i-la-pa-sra
Rampart, emma
Rapid, i-to
Rarely, pa-lis-ram
Raspberry, a-tw-na-tw-na
Rat, la-kas
Rather, mai-ke-to
Rattlesnake, war-pw-she
Rave, to, pa-lei-sha, na, ta, , tarnei
Raw, ra-pil
Reappear, pa-i-sha, pa-ish-na, pa-ish-ta, nmk, tarnei
Rear, anak
Receive, to, w-nep-sha, a, ta, k, tarnei
Recognize, to, shw-kwa-ni-sha
Red, (rouge), lw-cha, (roux), ma-resh
Reed, wa-pai
Regard, to, kré-nw-sha, na, ta, nk, tarnei, a-tok-sha, shana, ta, am, tarnei
Reject, to, w-ré-sha, a, ta, k, tarnei
Rejoin, to, pat-kw-ma-sha, na, ta, k, tarnei
Relate, to, ta-mwu-sha ta-lw-ak-sa
Relation, pen-min-ten
Remedy, plar, taw-ti-nwk
Remember, to, a-tem-na-nar-

sha, na, ta, k, tarnei, per-sha, na, ta, mk, tarnei

Render, *to,* pie-tor-sha, na, ta, mk, tarnei

Repast, *a,* t-kwa-tat

Repeat, *to,* sa-pw-in-sha, ka, ta, k, tarnei

Repent, *to,* nar-ti-sha-tem-na-pa

Reprehend, *to,* ti-a-nep-sha, pa, ta, k, tarnei.

Respect, *to,* te-mak-sha, ka, ta, om, tarnei

Retire, *to,* ei-keunk-sha, a, ta, om, tarnei

Return, *to,* é-tor-sha, na, ta, nmk, tarnei, tor-shamsh, tormna, tornemta, tornink, tarnei

Rib, ropt

Rich, ta-nw-eit-ié

Riches, ta-nw-eit

Rifle, krat-kati, tw-mi-pas

Right, t-sw-ei, t-kwik, *right side,* nw-it-kó-nik *Acc and dat* nw-it-kan

Ring, *a,* so-prol-kas

Ripe, ia-wié, a-ti-sha

Rise, *to,* tw-ti-sha, a, ta, k, tarnei, trak-shik-sha, a, ta, k, tarnei, *to rise again,* wa-krish-wi-sha, a, ta, k, tarnei

River, at-wan

Road, i-chet

Roast, *to,* ta-wa-sha, na, ta, k, tarnei

Robe (*of furs,*) she-moi, *an Indian woman's robe,* tap-ski

Robust, i-to, kol-tép

Rock, p-shwa

Root, met-sei, *an eatable root,* a-na-she

Rose, tam-she-shw-n-mi-na-tit

Rot, *to,* si-sw-sa, na, ta, k, tarnei

Route, i-chét

Rudder, w-shemtk

Rugged, krar

Run, *to,* wer-ti-sha, a, ta, k, tarnei, *to run to any one for interest,* wer-ti-o-sha, *to run a race,* sha-pa-la-wer-ti-sha, *to run away,* wi-na-nin-sha, a, ta, k, tarnei

Runner, wei-ti-tla

S.

Sack, ta-tash, le sac

Saddle, kla-kam

Saddle, *to,* kla-kam-i-sha, a, ta, om, tarnei

Salmon, *large,* t-kwi-nat, nwsor, *small,* ka-lor, é-sa, *white,* mé-tw-la

Salt, sol

Salt, *adj* so-lié

Salt, *to,* so-li-sa, a, ta, k, tarnei

Same, kws-ré

Sand, né-nw

Saturday, p-tar-nins-pa, o-i-lars-pa, sa-sa-pa-lw-i-tio

Savior, wa-krish-a-ni-tla

Saw, sar-kl-ka-was

Saw, *to,* sar-klek-sha, a, ta, om, tarnei

Scabbard, tw-shés

Scalp, to-ta-nik

Scarcely, ik-siks, wap-tai, mé-la

Scold, na-te-no-sha, na, ta, k, tarnei

Scratch, *to,* ws-kram-sha, na, ta, k, tarnei, pina-ei-a-sha

Sea, at-at-shes

Season, *to,* a-i-tw-a-sha, na, ta, k, tarnei

See, *to,* a-kré-nw-sha, na, ta, k, tarnei, a-tok-sha, a, ta, om, tarnei

Seek, to, a-wı-sha, a, ta, k, tarneı

Self, kws-re, né-nik at the end, himself, pen-ne-nik, ourselves, na-mak-ne-nik

Sell, to, ta-mı-a-sha, nu, ta, k, tarneı (neuter), pına before the verb

Send, to, mé-ta-sha, na, ta, k, tarneı, to send or go for, m-pa-ta-sha, na, ta, k, tarneı, to send back, e-to-ra-ta-sha, na, ta, k, tarneı

Separate, to, wı-a-pa-sha, na, ta, nk, tarneı

Set, to, the sun is setting, a-na-sha, na, ta, a-nas-kık-sha, a, ta, to set out, wı-na-sha, na, ta, k, tarneı

Seven, tws-ras, wı-nept

Seventy, tws-ras-tep-tıt, wı-nept-ıt

Several, lar-ma

Sew, to, wı-ser-sa, na, ta, k, tarneı

Shade, kresh

Shame, pı-na-klw-ı-at

Sharpen, to, sha-pa-tsam-sha, amka, ta, aınk, tarneı

She, peuk, pl pe-mak

Sheep, wa-o

Shelter, wa-w-twk-pa-ma, wa-w-twk-tesh

Ship, shep

Shirt, tat-pas, ta-rws-umı

Shiver, to, chw-eı-sha, na, ta, nem, tarneı, ı-o-ı-a-shak

Shoe, l-kram

Shot, small, ka-kıa-pa-ma

Shoulder, krem-kas

Shut, to, krap-a-kw-sha, ıa, ta, k, tarneı, to shut a door, w-esp-sa, a, ta, ak or a-sık, tarneı

Sick, pa-ıw-ı-tla

Sickness, pa-ıw, long, ta-ma-wa-tat

Side on this side, ché-nik

Sign, tı-mat

Silence! cho-tra-nak! w-sır! w-sr!

Silver, tā-la

Sin, che-lw-ıt-ıt, mel-la-wıt

Sin, to, mel-la-wı-sha, a, ta, k, tarneı, che-lwı-tı-sha

Since, a-na-ko, since when, mo-ma

Sing, to, w-emp-sha, a, ta, k, tarneı

Sister, (elder,) pat, younger, la-l-mwt, (named by brother,) at-se, (by sister) sı-pe, familiarly, nı-a

Sister-in-law, p-nok

Sit, to, aı-ık-sha, a, ta, aık, tarneı

Six, p-tar-nıns, o-ı-lars.

Sixteen, pw-tempt-wı-na-p-tar-nıns

Sixty, p-tar-nıns-p-tıt, o-ı-lars-p-tıt

Skin, é-par

Skin, to, shw-a-sha, shana, ta, k, tarneı

Skull, at-se-ra-sé-ras, pal-ka

Skunk, tı saı

Slander, to, ın-mo-sha, na, ta, k, tarneı

Slave, a-shw-a-nı-a

Sleep, pe-no, to go to sleep, pı-na-sha-pa-pe-no-sha, to put to sleep, sha-pa-pé-no-sha

Sleep, to, pe-no-sha, na, ta, nk, tarneı mam-rw-ı-sha, a, ta, nk, mam-w-sha, na, ta, nık, tarneı, to oversleep ones self in the morning, taw-kwm-sha, ma, ta, nık, tarneı, to sleep sound, me-kwet-pé-no-sha

Sleeper, one who goes to bed early, pe-no-ı-é, who rises late, taw-kwn-tla

Sleeve, kwa-ta-wı-as

Sloth, e-tok-wıt

Slothful, é-tok-tla
Slow, ai-a-i-ash
Smell, to, act nwk-shi-sha, a, ta, k, tarnei, neut ti-wa-sha
Smoke, la-teil-ke, la-ten-ke
Smoke, to, ta-wa-ri-sha, a, ta, k, tarnei, to-ré-sha
Snail, ras-lo
Snake, p-w-shé
Snore, to, tap-nor-sha, na, ta, k, tarnei
Snow, pw-i
Snow, to, pw-i-sha, na, ta, k, tarnei
Snowshoe, é-no
Soap, sa-pa-ir-a-was, sa-pa-i-rws
Soften, tla-war-anisha
Softly, tlw-ei
Soil, tet-sham
Some, some one, nars
Son, isht
Son-in-law, p-shés
Song, wem-pash
Soon, ké-to
Soul, ha-shw-it
Sound, to, (sonner), wa-tik-sha, a, ta, kom, tarnei
Soup, la soup, la kamine
Sour, plai, to be sour, skrw-lw-lam-sha, shana, ta, k, tarnei
Sourness, skrw-lw-tat
Sow, to, (plant), ta-ma-nik-sha, a, ta, om, tarnei
Spade, wa-po-i-kws-ta-tla, wa-ta-ta-was, wa-po-i-ka-was
Speak, to, na-twn-sha, na, ta, k, tarnei, esse-nwi-ssa, a, ta, k, tarnei
Spell, to cast a, wa-tei-i-sha, a, ta, k, tarnei
Spider, w-ral-ra-li
Spirit, wap-sor

Spit, to, ka-klik-sha, shana, ta, ink, tarnei
Spite, in spite of, kla-pré, n-chi-ké
Spittle, ka-kli-as
Split, a, wa-cher-ni
Split, to, wa-chei-sha, na, ta, nak, tarnei
Spoon, so-ras
Spot, ché-mak
Spring, wa-wa-rwm, wo-rwm
Sprinkle, to, i-a-ri-ka-sha-sha, na, ta, k, tarnei
Sprout, ta-war-sha, na, ta, k, tarnei
Spur, trap-ta-na-was
Squirrel, ni-sés, ground squirrel, le-mi-a
Stag, i-a-mash
Stallion, ta-la-ié
Stammer, to, em-ke-ka-wi-sha, a, ta, k, tarnei
Stammerer, em-k-kwa
Stand, to, up, tw-ti-sha, tra-chik-sha, ka, ta, k, tarnei
Star, ias-lo
Stark, klw-ei
Stay, to, at, tra-na-sha, w-sha-ik-sha
Steal, to, pa-rw-i-sha, a, ta, k, tarnei
Steel, sti, a steel to strike fire, tw-nis
Steer, to, a canoe, w-shemtk-sha, a, ta, k, tarnei
Stick, tw-kash
Stilts, wi-na-ta-was
Stink, to, i-la-ti-wu-sha, na, ta, k, tarnei
Stinking, si-sw
Stirrup, tw-na-kri-ka-was
Stocking, w-shi-aks
Stomach, na-wat, nwt
Stone, p-shw-a

Story, ta-mo, ta-lw-askt.
Stop, *to, act.* ei-krunk-sha, sha-na, ta, om, tarnei; *neut. for a moment,* tra-w-ser-sa, na, ta, k, tarnei; *forever,* w-ser-sa, na, ta, k, tarnei.
Stove, i-lat-shra-was.
Stranger, té-ner, shi-wa-nish.
Strangle, *to,* chaw-kre-sha, na, ta, k, tarnei.
Straw, shw-ist.
Strength, r-t-tw-it, kol-tep-wit.
Strike, *to,* ti-wi-sha, a, ta, k, tarnei.
Striped, tam-kla-ké, tam-a-kla-ké.
Strong, r-t-to, kol-tep.
Stubborn, kró-shem.
Such, sha-kwn, sho-a-shin.
Suffer, *to,* pa-i-w-wi-sha, a, ta, k, tarnei.
Sugar, shw-ker.
Summer, ré-mam, sha-tem.
Sun, an.
Sunrise, an-asha, an-atra.
Sunset, an-asht.
Sup, *to,* t-kwa-ta-sha, na, ta, k, tarnei.
Supple, tla-war.
Surely, nw-it-ka, kw-i-am.
Swallow, *to,* ne-krwn-sha, na, ta, kn, tarnei.
Sweat, lat-tlat.
Sweat, *to,* lat-tla-sha, na, ta, k, tarnei.
Sweating lodge, ro-i-aksh; *to take a sweat,* ro-i-aksha, a, ta, k, tarnei.
Sweet, tsi.
Swell, *to,* tet-sha, na, ta, k, tarnei; pw-la-sha, na, ta, k, tarnei.
Swim, *to,* sh-mw-ei-sha, ka, ta, k, tarnei.

T.

Table, ta-tla-elw-kas.
Tail, tw-in, ras-ros; *having a tail,* twin-ié.
Take, *to take away,* w-nep-sha, a, ta, k, tarnei.
Tallow, i-a-pash.
Tame, *to,* l-rat-a-nisha.
Taste, *to,* am-si-la-wi-sha.
Tattoo, *to,* pina-tra-wi-a-sha, na, ta, k, tarnei; *tattooed,* tra-wi-a-ni.
Tea, le thé.
Teach, *to,* sap-sw-kwa-sha, na, ta, k, tarnei.
Tear, il-pwl.
Tear, *to, (pluck away,)* tsa-rolk-sha, a, ta, om, tarnei.
Ten, pw-tempt.
Tent, nit, sil-haws.
That one, *(celui, celle,)* ana-pewk, *pl.* a-na-kw-mak, a-na-pe-mak.
The, nem *at the end of the word.*
Their, pé-mink.
Then, k-pailk, ana-charé.
There, i-kw-nak, kw-nak.
Therefore, kwn-kin.
They, pé-mak.
Thick, te-nw-pa-ham.
Thief, pa-rw-i-tlam.
Thing, ta-kwn, to-a-shin.
Think, *to think one's self,* pi-na-pri-na-sha, na, ta, k, tarnei
Thirst, ché-tat.
Thirsty, *to be,* ché-tasha, na, ta, k, tarnei.
Thirteen, pw-tempt-wi-na-mé-tat.
Thirty, mé-tap-tit.
This, ichi, iwk.
Thorn, tam-kwi-kwi.
Thou, imk, nam.

Thought, prwɪ-prwɪ, prw-ɪt
Thousand, pw-tap-pw-tɑp-tɪt
Thread, wɪs-ra-was, wɪs-rws
Three, mé-tat, *three persons,* mé-tao
Throat, em, nekrwash
Throw, *to,* w-ré-sha, na, ta, rɪnk, tarneɪ
Thunder, ɪ-nwn-tla
Thus, kws
Thy, é-mɪ-nɪk
Ticklish, tess
Timid, wɪ-é-chw-tla, skaw-tla, le-kok-tla
Tinder, lw-krwm
Tired, *to grow,* a-na-nw-wɪ-a-kw-sha, ɪa, ta, k, tarneɪ, pɪna-tkoe-sa-wɪ-sha
Tired, tkoeɪ-sa-wié
Tiresome, a-na-nwɪ-tla
Toad, a-lw-krat
Tobacco, ta-war, tor
To-day, wɪ-task, maké
Together, ko-ɪ-sɪm, lars-pa-sɪm, *you and I together,* na-pɪ-nɪk, *you and he together,* é-mɪ-ɪk
To-morrow, maɪsr, *day after to-morrow,* sra-maɪrs, maɪrs-pama-pa
Tongue, mé-lé-she
Tooth, é-tet
Tortoise, a-la-shɪk
Trace, wa-tɪksh
Trap, tɷk-she, twksh
Travel, *to,* wɪ-a-nɪn-sha, na, ta, k, tarneɪ
Traverse, *a,* ɪ-a-ro-ɪkt, ɪ-a-ro-ɪk-tesk
Tree, pe-teɪn, *large tree,* ark-sha
Trembling, wɪ-é-chw-nɪ
Trifle, *to, with one, make him lose a project,* tɪ-palé-ɪsha, shana, ta, k, tarneɪ

Trout, shw-sheɪns
True, nɪw-ɪt-ka, kw-ɪ-am
Tunic, shé-mor
Twenty, nep-tɪt
Twice, na-pam
Twist, *to,* te-ke-nɪ-sha, a, ta, k, tarneɪ

U.

Ugly, chaw-shɪr
Umbrella, tor-tor-pa-ma
Uncle, pɪɪr, pɪmɪr
Unconquered, wa-sha-nal
Under, ra-lok, *gen* ché-nɪk, *acc and dat* chen *From beneath,* ra-lok-pa-ma, ra-lok-tlɪ-ma
Understand, *to,* ɪ-ɪk-sha, a, ta, nem, tarneɪ
Understockings, w-shɪ-aks
Ungrateful, tem-na-nwt
Unhandy, chaw-wap-sor
Unreflecting, chaw-prw-ɪnɪ
Up, *upright,* tw-tɪé, tw-tɪk, tra-chɪk
Upon, pa *at the end of the word*
Urine, cws
Useless, a-w-tɪ-ka, at-shɪ-na

V.

Vain, chel-chel
Vase, twk-saɪ
Vast, n-chɪ
Vein, a-kweɪ-sa-kwsh
Vermilion, pɪ-lw-et, sa-pe-ɪn-ches
Very, n-nenk *at the end of the word*
Vile, chɪ-a-w-o
Violet, lw-cha
Virgin, te-maɪ
Visible, kré-nw-nɪ

Vomit, *to*, chip-shi-sha, a, ta, k, tarnei

W.

Wadding, ta-kwn-te-tesh
Wadhook, *(ramrod screw,)* sko-la-pa-was
Waistcoat, wa-krel-pi
Wait for, *to*, wa-krict-sha, ka, ta, kom, tarnei, i-a-rwa-sha, na, ta, k, tarnei, é-mw-iak-sha, a, ta, k, tarnei é-mw-iak-sha, a, ta, k, tarnei, *to wait a long while*, ta-ma-w-a-ré-sha, shana, ta, k, tarnei
Walk, *to take a*, wi-a-nin-sha, na, ta, k, tarnei
Want, wei-a-wit
War, pi-at-nat, pi-kli-a-wit
Warm, la-rw-ir
Warm, *to*, *one's self*, la-sé-moi-sa, ia, ta, k, tarnei
Wash, *to*, a-sha-pa-ir-sha, na, ta, nink, tarnei, *the face*, she-men-ta-sha, na, ta, k, tarnei, *the hands*, wa-bi-a-sha, na, ta, k, tarnei
Wasp, wi-twi-nat
Watcher, kro-lem
Water, t-tshes, t-shws, *to make water*, e-ws-pi-sha, a, ta, k, tarnei
Wave, a-mw-i
We, na-mak, na-ma, *ue two*, na-man
Weak, shw-krat-ni, sha-law, lk-kap
Wearisomeness, a-na-nwi-wit
Weary, tkoei-sa-wie, *to be weary of*, a-na-nw-wi-sha, a, ta, k, tarnei
Weep, nar-ti-sha, a, ta, k tarnei
Weeping, nar-ti-é
West, ws-la-sé-ikt

Wet, *to*, i-akl-pi-sha, a, ta, k, tarnei
What, twn, mish
Wheat, a-i-ta-lo
When, mwn, *since when*, mo-ma
Whence, mé-nik
Where, main, mé-nan
Which, a-na-pe-uk
Whip, wa-ta-na-was
Whip, *to*, wa-ta-sha, na, ta, k, tarnei
Who ? shin ? *who is there ?* shin-iwa-kw-nak
Whortleberry, wi-w-no, a-tit
Why, tei, tw-iei, tw-iao
Wife, a-sham
Wig, to-ia-nik
Wind, w-kri, w-li, *to be windy*, w-kri-sha, w-li-sha, a, ta, k, tarnei, *to break wind*, tit-sha, na, ta, k, tarnei
Window, kré-nw-ta-was
Winter, anem
Winter, *to*, a-nw-é-mi-sha, a, ta, k, tarnei
With *is rendered by* ik *or* in *at the end of the word*
Wolf, *large*, la-la-wish, ra-lish, *small*, spi-li-é
Woman, a-i-ct, ti-la-ki
Wood, e-lw-kas, *to cut wood*, sar-kl-cha, ka, ta, kom, tarnei
Wood, *wooden*, e-lw-kasn-mi
Woody, e-lw-kas-ié
Wool, la-o-la-o
Word, na-twn, es-sé-nw-it, té-lat, *one word*, sre-té-lat
Work, kwt-kwt
Work, *to*, kwt-kwt-sha, ia, ta, k, tarnei
Wormwood, pesh-ro
Wound *with a gun*, *to*, a-tor-na-sha, na, ta, k, tarnei, *with a knife*, p-ti-a-sha, na, ta, k, tarnei, *with a*

stick, &c, sap-né-ik-sha, a, ta, ik, tarnei, *wound one's self is rendered by* pi-na *before the verb*, pi-na-tor-na-sha, &c

Wound, *a,* a-tor-nat, p-ti-at, sap-né-ikt, pa-i-wit

Write, *to,* ti-ma-sha, na, ta, k, tarnei

Y.

Yard, tc-tar-she

Year, pwi, an-w-im, an-w-ikt, an-w-isht

Yellow, ma-resh, par

Yes, é

Yesterday, kla-wit, wa-tim, *day before yesterday,* sra-kla-wit, w-a-tim-pama

You, i-mak, pam, mates

Your, ma-mink

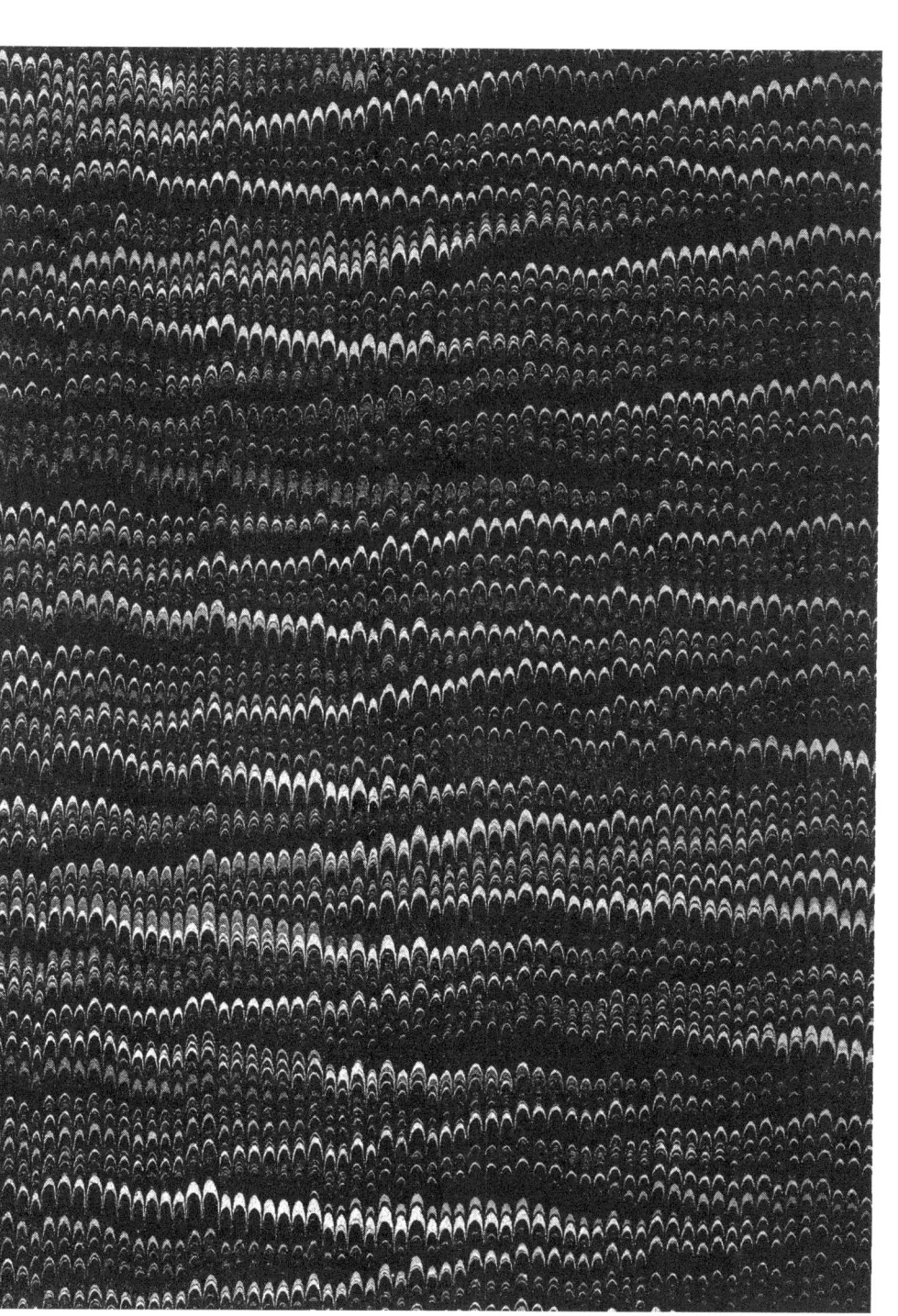

CPSIA information can be obtained
at www.ICGtesting.com
Printed in the USA
LVHW042112100323
741353LV00012B/839